I0796298

Praise for *Church Camp*

"This evocative book is an elegy over white evangelical church camp culture from one who was once among the leaders of this multibillion-dollar industry. *Church Camp* deconstructs the theology and culture of this industry, making it a significant contribution to the comprehensive reconsideration of white evangelicalism currently taking place. Highly recommended!"

David P. Gushee, author of *The Moral Teaching of Jesus*

"As someone who has spent many years wrestling through the scattered carnage of my own experiences with white evangelicalism, I didn't realize how important it was for me to hear this particular story told in this particular way. If you've experienced church camp from the 'inside'—either as a camper or as a staff person or (as is the case for most of us) both, I cannot recommend *Church Camp* highly enough. I want to get it in the hands of everyone I shared that experience with, to give us a chance to voice what was troubling *and* to consider how to live into a different way of experiencing the sacred together."

Jessica Floyd, therapist and former camp program staff

"Speaking the familiar language of chilly mornings and muggy days, *Church Camp* peels back the nostalgia and shines light on both the fruit and the flaws of an evangelical rite of passage. Through personal experience and detailed research, Cara Meredith points toward faith formation that refuses shame, squashes fear, and embraces hope in the mystery. This book is for every camper who fought to belong or started asking better questions. It is for anyone who wants to sit in the warmth of God's unconditional goodness."

Shannan Martin, author of *Start with Hello* and *The Ministry of Ordinary Places*

"*Church Camp* captures the feelings and love that camp life engenders, but then asks the hard questions about the institution itself. Cara Meredith doesn't shy away from writing about complicated subjects that plague modern religion and camp: race, gender, and ultimately if evangelicalism is even a viable path forward. I found it to be a surprising page-turner and read it in one sitting, intrigued by the structure of following a week at camp, entertained throughout, and curious from start to finish. I absolutely recommend this book to anyone who ever set foot in a summer camp."

Buren Renick III, COO and former senior camp counselor

"I spent many childhood summers in the colorful, complicated world Cara Meredith describes so deftly in this thoughtful and searingly honest book. I remember the gooey s'mores, the starlit hikes, the cheesy skits—and the powerful, quietly insidious culture of white evangelicalism that undergirded the whole experience, especially for those of us who attended church camp as children of color. Meredith doesn't shy away from this insidiousness; she exposes and dismantles it. Using the very words and stories she once shared so earnestly with children during her years as a camp speaker, she describes a religious subculture bent on priming and converting children not simply to Christianity but to the cultural norms, beliefs, and assumptions of white American evangelicalism. She describes who benefited from this endeavor, and who got hurt. Who found faith, and who lost it. Most importantly, Meredith shares her own journey of an evolving and nuanced spirituality—one that allows her to remember church camp as a sacred place that formed her in so many beautiful ways, even as she also grieves over the God it misrepresented, the culture it perpetuated, and the children it harmed. This is a searching and necessary book—a testimony to the power of telling hard, healing truths about the places we have loved."

Debie Thomas, author of *A Faith of Many Rooms* and *Into the Mess and Other Jesus Stories*

"With humor and tenderness, just as Cara tells my story, I am confident she describes many of your stories too. Readers should prepare to measure their own experiences as they sift through the pages of *Church Camp*, entirely because Cara brilliantly paints and weaves her own church camp life alongside many of ours."

Joey Lynne, business owner; former camper and counselor

"If I could trade attending church fifty-two times a year and attending church camp for one week per year, I'm pretty sure I'd pick camp. That's how powerful camp experience was in my spiritual and human upbringing. But it would not be the kind of camp I grew up with. It would be the kind of camp Cara Meredith points to in her book *Church Camp*. This book tells the truth about what's wrong with conventional Christian camps while celebrating the undiscovered promise camping holds for those who dare to seize it."

Brian D. McLaren, author of *Do I Stay Christian?* and *Faith After Doubt*

"Cara Meredith tackles the topic of evangelical church camp—something so many of us deeply love and are also deeply wounded by—with bravery, kindness, and incisive truth-telling. Her experiences resonate with those of us who spent decades of our lives working in Christian camping: we loved it but didn't understand at the time the damage it was doing, and many of us have now come to realize it was incredibly problematic. Cara handles these issues with an unwavering honesty, inviting us to reexamine why we held church camp dear and to advocate for a more inclusive, Christ-centered way forward. If you grew up attending or working at this type of camp, I recommend that you read this book."

Holly Hoeksema, professional development coach; former camp director and camp speaker

"It's rare to find a book that's capable of holding the tension of the both/and when it comes to the sacred, but Cara Meredith has accomplished just that in her newest release, *Church Camp.* As a former church camp kid, I experienced a flood of memories upon reading, during which I found myself both laughing and nodding in agreement. This book will not only help you reminisce about the past; it will spur you to dream about what the future could be."

Jonathan Merritt, award-winning columnist and author of *Learning to Speak God from Scratch*

"If you grew up in white evangelicalism, you probably had an experience at a Christian camp of some sort. In *Church Camp,* Cara Meredith does a magnificent job of meshing the historical view of this phenomenon alongside personal insights to normalize and maybe even move on from these sometimes utterly bizarre experiences. I highly recommend!"

Kurt Kroon, co-pastor at Cascade Church Portland and former camp program director

"In *Church Camp,* Cara Meredith transports me to the world of so many of my own summers. Beautiful settings in the mountains, the buzz and energy of a group of young people in a place set apart for something special, late-night conversations about a world-shattering faith. Walking us through the fascinating subculture that is a staple of evangelical Christianity, Cara does not hold back from the historical, critical, and theological in her weaving together a variety of first-person narratives with song lyrics and the sequence of familiar talks. She shows us the hidden but not always subtle entanglements of whiteness and privilege in the overarching project around conversion. But Cara offers, too, a surprising and different way into an experience — with all its flaws and quirkiness — that might actually tell us something surprising about humanity. She gives a glimpse in the prologue: '...it's a book about the tenacity of plain old human beings like you and me who learn how to hold on tight to a thing called hope.' So grateful for the immense thoughtfulness and care in this work."

Mihee Kim-Kort, author of *Outside the Lines: How Embracing Queerness Will Transform Your Faith*

Church Camp

CHURCH CAMP

BAD SKITS, CRY NIGHT, & HOW WHITE EVANGELICALISM BETRAYED A GENERATION

CARA MEREDITH

Broadleaf Books
Minneapolis

CHURCH CAMP
Bad Skits, Cry Night, and How White
Evangelicalism Betrayed a Generation

29 28 27 26 25 24 1 2 3 4 5 6 7 8 9

Library of Congress Control Number: 2024033703 (print)

Cover design: Broadleaf Books

Print ISBN: 979-8-8898-3100-6
eBook ISBN: 979-8-8898-3101-3

Printed in China.

To Michael Weldon and Sarah Powell,
two camp friends who changed the story for me

Contents

Prologue

In the summer of 2014, my faith became a fraud. When my friend Brian had asked me to speak at camp seven or eight months earlier, my fingers couldn't type back a quick enough response: *Yes, I want to speak at camp again! I'm honored you would ask! Thank you!* Exclamation points to his invitation became my love language, excitable punctuation marks dotting the end of every sentence in reply. In more ways than one, this felt like the only appropriate response, the only thing I could say upon being asked.

Camp, and that camp in particular, had been such a formative part of my own journey—a storied collection of playfulness, joy, and acceptance and, later, of sadness, anger, and doubt, all coming together to weave a collective tale of becoming. Camp was the place I felt most at home, the place where the most authentic version of me came out to play. It was the place I became my silliest and, perhaps, most real self: I donned brightly colored Hawaiian muumuus and baseball hats with pig snouts sewn onto the bill from the costume closet. I belted out songs about how King Jesus is all, armpits sweaty from the complicated, accompanying motions. Camp was the place I most deeply felt the presence of God, where nature offered a peek into the holy, if you were just willing to open your eyes and see. The greens of the willow trees and the browns of the towering redwoods spoke a calming peace; rolling hills, dotted by a hundred different trail combinations, lay scattered against a faultless backdrop of cerulean skies. There was no place on earth quite like this sacred playground—and somehow it was almost as if this very place had chosen me in return.[1] The essence of my faith, my story, my very being, camp was the epitome of *me.*

When Brian emailed me, I didn't seem to remember the hard parts, at least not yet. Instead, I cast my lot on memories of good, as if the eternal optimist in me could hardly stand to see a scrape of gray cloud in the periwinkle sky. After all, the essence of camp wasn't just something I felt inside; it was also something I had *done* on the outside, as a camper and, later, as a staff member. Some might say I rose up the ranks of church camp when, over the course of nearly two decades, I held the following jobs at a variety of different camps, no less:

- Cleanup crew
- Kitchen staff
- Lifeguard
- Ropes course instructor
- Camp counselor
- Head counselor (or leader)
- Program team
- Musician
- Speaker

In more ways than one, *camp* was who I'd always been. Camp defined me. Camp gave me life, for camp *was* ultimate life to me. Until it wasn't anymore.

The story, or part of it, at least, goes like this: In the span of time between Brian's invitation to speak at camp and me actually showing up *to* speak at camp, a couple of things happened. First, I found out I was pregnant with my second son. All joy and excitement aside, the pregnancy proved harsh on my body. By the time spring rolled around, I woke up at two or three every morning, middle and lower back crippled in pain. Insomnia would kick in, and I would migrate from the bed to a heap of blankets on the floor, body desperate for sleep while my mind begged me to stay awake and unravel perceived mysteries of life. This didn't make caring for my older son, a mere toddler, any easier. The lack of sleep and constant, ongoing pain didn't help my dreams of trying to succeed as a writer either. I wondered if I'd gotten it all wrong, if I'd made a mistake in leaving the traditional workforce the year before to pursue a writing career. Was all of this chasing-after a meaningless, empty pipe dream? In all of these places, God felt far away, or at least far from the confines of plastic sippy cups, afternoon nap schedules, and countless trips to the neighborhood playground. *Are you there, God? It's me, Cara*, I remember thinking to myself while channeling the title of one of my favorite childhood books. Lying awake in the predawn hours, there were often more questions than answers. *Why have you left me all alone? Is this all there is now? What am I even doing here anymore?*

Because that's when a second thing happened: Disillusionment started to creep in. My faith started to feel like a counterfeit bill. I joked to my writing pals that entire chapters were penned during that third watch of the night, when I lay awake on a scraggly heap of blankets. But in a way, they were. I'd started writing what I hoped would become my first book, a spiritual memoir about my experiences as a woman in ministry, as a new mother, and as someone who felt like she had lost her way when the two worlds collided. Entire plot lines flickered dimly in those early-morning hours. Stories I hadn't thought about for ten, twenty years flooded back into my mind. Bleary-eyed, I'd scribble midnight revelations onto scraps of paper or into the notes section on my cell phone. Some of those words became entire chapters, others fodder for the recycling basket.

In the end, that book didn't end up being anything but a seventy-seven-thousand-word manuscript that showed me I could write a book, if I really tried hard enough. But those midnight revelations and all the accompanying questions birthed something else in me, something beyond the embryo-turned-fetus growing inside my body. Those revelations birthed doubt.

Everything that had once felt so true—especially of that place called *camp*—didn't feel so easy and clear, so black and white anymore. God felt like less a connect-the-dots puzzle and more like a haphazard collection of dots flung across the room toward me. *Here, try and put this together!* Left without a clue as to direction, let alone an example two- or three-dimensional picture, I didn't know where to start. When Brian announced he was leaving his position a month or two before I was scheduled to speak at camp, I thought about tendering my resignation too. It had been a few years since I'd been a speaker and nearly a decade and a half since I'd spent the summer as a seasonal staff employee. I felt old, expired, well past the desired shelf life of someone who should be hanging out at camp again for the week.

But I would only be there for a week, I reasoned. Everything would be fine. So I didn't send an email. I didn't ask them to find another speaker, and I didn't tell them I would be nearly eight months pregnant when I took the stage. Part of me didn't want to give the new hiring director a reason *not* to extend any future invitations: If I didn't take the gig, what if another opportunity to speak never came around again? I rallied against the assumption that I'd left a job in ministry to become a stay-at-home mom, but when invitations to speak dried up and my name was no longer tied to a Christian organization, I wondered if I'd gotten it all wrong. If I could just be my very campy self once again, I thought, then I could fulfill the dream. I could prove I hadn't been wrong, that *this* really was where I was supposed to be. But camp wasn't my home anymore. Camp wasn't *me* anymore, not if all those midnight revelations and doubts about God had anything to say about it.

When June rolled around, I stood on stage, belly sticking out nearly a foot from my midsection. I tried to tell all the old stories, the ones that found me bouncing and jumping across the creaky wooden stage, enraptured laughter the only response from the other side. But I was out of breath, my sentences short—staccato notes stuck into the middle of a rolling concerto. I waddled from one side of the platform to the other, unable to tell stories like I wanted to tell them, unable to herald the God I was being paid to proclaim.

Maybe the most fraudulent piece of all was that I could barely say the word *God*, at least not that week. I could say *Jesus*, if I was reading a text, but in the aftermath of explanations and stories and invitations, my mouth could not regurgitate anything else. *Lord* was out of the question, *Father* not even comprehensible. I couldn't say those names because I didn't know what I believed anymore.

Sometimes I find myself throwing pennies into a wishing well of memories: If only I'd been more transparent, honest about the real rumblings of my soul. If only I'd been gentler with the new version of a less-campier me, even if the Really Real emerged a little different on the other side of it all.[2] What if I had told those middle school campers the truth? *I'm scared, friends.* Scared my upside-down bowl of spiritual Jell-O self will never be made right again. Jiggle that thing too much, and she's going to come crashing, slopping, sliding down to the kitchen floor. But give her time to breathe and sit and ruminate in silence, and maybe she'll show up for the after-church potluck again sometime soon.

I guess I didn't yet know that some things require a little more time.

/ / /

If you've picked up this book, chances are camp holds a special place in your heart—even if it's a place you now feel like burning down to the ground. For those of us who grew up in white, evangelical spaces, church camp was a natural part of the calendar year. We had back-to-school Sunday school kickoffs in September, orange-and-brown-themed harvest events in the fall, and candlelit Christmas Eve services in December. Churches pulled out all the stops on Easter Sunday, but it was anyone's guess what happened in April and May when sports schedules ramped up and the sun peeked out from behind winter clouds. By the time June, July, and August rolled around, the Sunday school teachers and youth group leaders needed a break. Time to hop on the bus for camp, kids!

To many of us, church camp was Kanakuk Kamps and Cowboy's Rest. It was Camp Pinnacle and T Bar M, Camp Arrah Wanna and Camp Minnesota. For some of us, camp happened through Young Life and YFC, FCA, and CRU Summer Missions, even when some folks in the camping world debated whether *those* camps could really be called *church camps* at all.[3] These were the places indelibly printed in our minds—the holy, outdoor spaces that changed us and marked our childhoods. It was like the Big Guy upstairs had poked a giant finger down to that one, special pinprick of a spot on the map. Because when you sang all those campy, lame songs and whispered the prayers and made the kinds of decisions you could only make at camp, a special kind of mountaintop high became the only accompaniment. Loving God was easy at camp; being a good Christian felt pretty simple too. Syrupy counselors wanted to know you. Perfect strangers loved to shout your name from across the sports field. Grown-ups considered gooey, dripping s'mores an utterly normal part of your daily diet.

And that's the thing: There was nothing like a week at church camp, even if the real test came when we got home and were faced with the *things of this world*. When temptations like *90210* and Nirvana and belly button T-shirts smacked us in the face, we forgot about daily rhythms of worship music and spending time with God.[4] The normalcies of camp seemed to vanish into thin air; the ease of prayer went away. It was easy to love God when everyone around us was loving God too—when chins dropped like holy automatons, down to the chest in prayer, and when hands inched upward toward the sky, we couldn't help but do the same. But when we got home from camp, we felt alone. When we weren't in that place, surrounded by those people, singing those songs, we forgot all about it. Until the next summer, that is, when the cycle started all over again.

Of course, some of us didn't want the cycle to ever stop, though. When we no longer qualified as campers, we became summer staff workers and year-round employees. We found our way back to camp, back to that magical spot where God and nature kiss.

I guess I became one of those people too. Halfway through my freshman year of college, I realized I needed to find a summer job, so I went to the career counselor for advice.[5] I don't remember our conversation as much as I remember her lugging a four-inch binder down from the high and crowded shelf behind her desk and shoving it across the table toward me. *SUMMER CAMPS* had been scrawled across the front cover, as if by a thick black Sharpie, inside sections organized by tabs according to state. I thumbed through the A and B states before pausing on the letter C: *I'll go to California*, I thought. *It's not too far away. It's a pretty cool place.* My attention span (and my decision-making) equivalent to the life expectancy of a mayfly,[6] I caught sight of a marigold pamphlet with quirky font and lighthearted humor: that camp in the Santa Cruz mountains became my top choice, the only place I wanted to spend fourteen weeks of my summer. I printed out an application in the computer lab a couple of hours later and, as luck would have it, hitched a ride to northern California several months later.

For the next twenty years, church camp became my destiny, the place I was meant to go and the person I was meant to be. I spent four summers in college working at that same marigold pamphlet of a camp, first as a ropes course instructor and then as part of the program team. When I became a high school English teacher, I couldn't escape camp during the lean and quiet months of summer. It was like the place pulsed through my blood. I kept on coming back, this time as a camp speaker. Speaking at one camp turned into an invitation from another, and eventually another, and soon took up the majority of my time outside of the classroom, on the weekends and during the summer months. An insistence toward the ways of camp didn't stop when I started working for an international youth outreach organization after four years in the classroom. In more ways than one, camp had been built into the ethos of the ministry: As staff, we regularly took teenagers to camp throughout the school year and again in June, July, and August. We showed up at camp to be trained and to train and, later, to staff these same camps as speakers and musicians, program teams and managers.

Year after year, in all of those places called *camp*, I interacted with thousands of children and youth. In spaces deemed hallowed and holy, I showed up and gave it my all. There, I felt most alive, tapped into the God I believed wholly present on those grounds. Perhaps it's only fitting that church camp would become the place where I came to the edge. No longer able to make sense of it all, camp was where I began to tear apart my faith.

/ / /

Within my body, church camp has housed my greatest joy and my greatest grief. Nowhere have I felt more alive, more in tune with the presence of God. And nowhere have I also mourned the damage done to others and the damage done to me, too often in the name of Jesus—for the things we thought *stood* for Jesus—as we sheltered under the umbrella of white evangelicalism. Church camp has been the source of some of my deepest hurts, just as it has been the foundation of some of the sincerest kindnesses and generosities I have ever known. I have been publicly ridiculed, mocked, and doubted; I have wept for the names called me and the assumptions made about me; I have mourned the loss of relationships, of those I once thought would be around forever. But I whisper these words alongside the truth that camp has also been a rock of genuine goodwill and bounty to me, a place I felt most at home and applauded for my gifts, a place that made me want to be a better person. Camp shaped me into the human I am today, even if I sometimes wish I could hit the rewind button a couple thousand times.

As it goes, I critique that place called *camp* because I love that place called *camp*. In a speech about the Vietnam War, Dr. King said, "I criticize America because I love her. I want her to stand as a moral example to the world."[7] To many, he "remained a rebellious lover of the country,"[8] even as he exposed her wrongs and held her to a higher, better standard. Perhaps it's not so different for us now, when it comes to the conversation at hand and to this microcosm of white evangelicalism. I think about how some of us are just starting to make connections between the old and the new, between who we were as children and who we have become as adults. I suppose it's not all that different for me, at least not when it comes to the girl who once called church camp the greatest place on earth and the woman who doesn't know if she can send her own kids there now. What do we do when a middle way isn't clear? How do we hold the tension of two opposite things existing at the very same time?

I imagine many of us find ourselves in this place of tension, when the things that made sense ten, twenty, or thirty years ago no longer hold up. In white evangelical church camp settings, exclusion doesn't make sense—not of my brothers and sisters of color, not of the LGBTQ+ community, and not of women. Making kids feel like shit in order to understand God's love for them doesn't make sense either, and neither do values of manipulation and capitalism; violent and bloody depictions of the cross; magical, saving prayers; and golden tickets to a faraway place called *heaven*. In this small paragraph alone, I imagine a fair number of readers will no doubt wonder if this is just another story of faith deconstruction: I suppose in some ways it is. Even though this is mostly a story of camp, it's also a story of rethinking previously held beliefs and imagining new ways forward. It's a story of asking "why?" over and over again. I imagine none of that would have happened without a spiritual evolution on my part.

Lest you begin to believe this is a story about me, though, it isn't. Church camp has never just been about me. Instead, it's about the hundreds of thousands of campers who attend camp every summer and those of us who found a home in the church camps of our youth. It's about those who dedicated their lives to camping ministries and those who refuse to set foot on their grounds again. It's about women and men and humans who do not align with a single gender; it's about people of color and white folks; it's about gay and straight, queer and nonbinary. It's about the religious and the nonreligious, about those who identify as evangelical and those who find a home in smells and bells and prayers prayed by a thousand tongues for thousands of years. It's about those who run far away from any sort of spiritual label and those who wonder if a god or gods even exist at all, even if they once stood on stage, proclaiming the virtues of a holy, triune God.

It's about the nearly fifty individuals I had the honor of interviewing over the course of a year and a half, many of whose stories you'll find in the pages of this book. It's about Tiffany, who reminded me that God is not a male, and Harmony, who was banned from camp property when they came out as bisexual. It's about Jeff, who took a risk in wondering whether belonging comes before belief, and Andrew, who saw the capitalistic mess of camp and wondered if there might be another way forward. It's about the interviewees who are not named but whose stories dot the Is and cross the Ts on every single page of this book.

Maybe it's also a story about you.

/ / /

At its core, this is a book about church camp. As any story often goes, though, the core subject matter also acts as a springboard into bigger, deeper conversations within faith and culture, justice and theology. I tell this layered story in seven sections as a nod to the progression of seven standard talks I used to give as a camp speaker:

- Night 1: Welcome to Camp!
- Night 2: God the Mostly Father
- Night 3: Superhero Jesus
- Night 4: Dirty Rotten Little Sinners
- Night 5: Cry Night
- Night 6: Side Note, Rose Again
- Night 7: Now Go and Live the (White) Way of Jesus

As you might imagine, most of these titles have changed a bit over the years, but the seven sections remain the tent pegs that anchor my little tabernacle of a story to the ground. After all, in the white evangelical church camp world, the progression shares somewhat of a universal quality that children and youth generally hear during the week at camp. In a way, you could say each chapter loosely follows the same progression: what I said, what was wrong with what I said, and what we could say instead. The point is not to focus on words I once proclaimed from the stage but to look at the intention and the implications within a culture and theology of white evangelicalism that exist behind my words. These points will largely be proven by stories from different interviewees, as well as through a hybrid sort of writing that includes elements of journalism, memoir, and research.

When it comes to the stories featured in the pages of this book, you'll get to know folks from a variety of Protestant and evangelical backgrounds, including nondenominational, Southern Baptist Convention (SBC), and Presbyterian camps, to name a few, as well as individuals from parachurch organizations such as Young Life and FCA (Fellowship of Christian Athletes). I remain profoundly grateful to each and every interviewee who gave me forty-five minutes (to two and a half hours, in one case) of their time. While much of this tome largely draws from my own story, I can only hope it is also the story of so many other people. I have additionally drawn heavily from the writings of Christians ranging from Nadia Bolz-Weber (Lutheran), to Walter Brueggemann (United Church of Christ), to Richard Rohr (Roman Catholic), as well as to authors like Tricia Hersey and Christena Cleveland, whose denominational preferences are not so easily determined.

This book is titled *Church Camp* for obvious reasons: it's about the institution of white evangelical church camps in America. Just as church camp is a magical place that shaped and formed so many of us, it's also a place just as many have had to bid a fond farewell to in the last several years. Far from inclusive toward wide swaths of humanity who have not been offered belonging on its grounds, it's time some of us listen to the stories of those whose voices have not always been heard—including of those who have often been excluded from campfire pits and sports arenas at the hands of prejudice and hate. Sometimes, though, this is simply a book about a God who lets things die and then makes them come back to life; it's a book about the tenacity of plain old human beings like you and me who learn how to hold on tight to a thing called *hope*. It's about our young and our old selves, about the prayers we prayed and the games we played; it's about camp romances found in a matter of three days or less and the squeezy cheese we stuffed into our mouths during cabin time.

As you read these words, I trust you'll learn something new about this facet of Christian subculture that is so prevalent and deeply impactful, even if it has yet to be explored in depth. I imagine the stories present on these pages will make you think and feel; I bet you might even chuckle a time or two if luck (and an ounce or two of snark and wit) has anything to do with it. More than anything, though, I hope you'll find yourself back in a land of cowboy cabins, roaring campfires, and endless choruses that always sound best when sung under a blanket of stars.

Welcome to church camp!

1

Welcome to Camp!

We didn't waste any time on Night One. As a speaker, my job was to get straight to the point, to help campers realize I had something they needed to hear. I welcomed them to that place called *camp*, pointing out the obvious: not only were they surrounded by hundreds of other really good-looking humans, such as themselves, but all those really good-looking humans (such as themselves) were about to embark on the *best* week of their lives. Sometimes I also told them a little story about the lone Black man sitting in the far back corner, a man whom I happened to call my husband.

I probably said something like this: "Now, campers, after James and I had been dating for a few months, he decided it was time for me to meet the family. *This* was a really big deal, like a Really Big Deal with a capital RBD. But we did it. We said yes. The two of us hopped on a plane on our way to Jackson, Mississippi; after we landed, we got in a rental car and drove twenty minutes down the road to a little gray house. It was time to meet his parents, James and Judy, and all the other Js: his sister, Jessica; and her four kids, Janae, Jameria, Jaylah, and little baby James."

Although the night was far from theologically meaty, I likely talked about how nervous I felt in the moment, how my heart was beating like a big, bad drum—a *pa-pum, pa-pum, pa-pum* so loud it must have leapt out of my chest, straight onto the outsides of pale white skin.

But then I told them about the welcome we experienced in the little gray house—a welcome sung by a chorus of shouts that felt like enveloping hugs for the uncle they ached to see. "Have you ever been somewhere and immediately felt right at home?" I probably asked them. I wanted to connect with the campers; I wanted the anecdote to stir something inside them, something to make them feel right at home.

But the real climax of the talk came when I began to tell a tale of playing hide-and-go-seek with the nieces and nephews. Even though I sat in Granddaddy's recliner, closing my eyes and counting a drawn-out *one Mississippi, two Mississippi, three Mississippi*, all the way up to thirty *Mississippi*, the unimaginable happened when I yelled out, "Ready or not, here I come!"

A little voice chirped out, "Ready!" And then another, and another, and another too: "Ready!" "Ready!" "Ready!" The chirping children had given away their sacred hiding spots. The little birds had made themselves known.

This, of course, allowed me to make a critical point, both about the illustrative story and about the campers who sat on concrete steps around the campfire pit, on wooden benches surrounded by swirling strands of switchgrass, or on a polypropylene carpet in a grand, wooden clubroom: These children were *ready* in Mississippi, I must have emphasized. They couldn't wait to be *found* in Mississippi. These young ones played a different kind of hide-and-go-seek: they played a game of wanting to be found.

I could only hope the parallel was obvious: Some of us were hiding. Some of us were just waiting, asking, hoping to be found. And many of us, no matter where we are on our respective spiritual journeys, would be found that week at camp.

Because for all of us, this was a story of being found.

/ / /

But for the prayer, the names *God* and *Jesus* were never uttered in the first night's talk. They didn't have to be because, as the one whose feet proclaimed the gospel, the invitation to enter into all that lay ahead was more than enough. After all, the first night of camp was always the most thrilling and ecstatic, an evening kept afloat with a pious kind of sex appeal and accompanying nods to the Holy Spirit.

"If sex appeal can infiltrate the Christian camping scene," one interviewee recalled, "then it was like the apostle Paul himself preached the gospel in a strapless corset teddy, bunny ears, and black sheer-to-waist pantyhose on the first night of camp!" I laughed at his description, crass as it may sound. But he was right: We pulled out all the stops. We gave it our all in an effort to show campers they really were going to have the best week of their lives. We shouted it into the microphone. We sang it in our songs. No matter our role, we rallied, we performed, we ushered our audiences into buying what only we alone could offer.

The invitation for campers to ready themselves for the next six days—relationally, physically, and spiritually—was presented through story, laughter, and an electric kind of energy. As a speaker, my entire job was to establish trust: like a many-armed octopus, all eight of my proverbial appendages sought to reach down from the stage and suction on to each one of those little camper hearts.

Along the way, I would become their guide. I would establish a case for Christ. Following a prescribed set of themes already laid out before me, I knew my whole goal was to lead them toward an affirmative answer to a single question: *Will you say yes to God's invitation?* However it came across, I stood on stage, flapping my arms and telling my stories and animating my face entirely so campers could come to a place of realization and knowing, beyond a shadow of a doubt, that Jesus had died on the cross for them and them alone. Because at some point during the week, they would be asked to respond to an invitation of faith.

Conversion, after all, was the entire point.

But before we tackle the language of conversion, we have to examine the role of the converter. The word *converter* is an agent noun (a noun derived from a verb) of the word *convert*. First recorded in the 1530s, the word wouldn't be associated with appliances or electronic devices for another three hundred years; instead, its sole connotation was to its parent action, to "a change or turn from one religion to another."[1] The role of the converter was to win over and change, to turn around and bend and transform. And the role of the converter, as it turns out, was almost always associated with a turn toward the Christian religion.[2]

In a recent video from the popular Instagram account Pastor Humor, a clean-cut white man gives a four-sentence statement about planning for the upcoming Easter services. Biceps bulge out of a tight purple shirt, a flesh-colored mic lapel strung across his cheek. The presumed pastor looks straight into the camera and addresses his staff: "I need drama. I need commitment. I need performance. I need production value . . . from you."[3]

A Celine Dion song plays in the background, and every sentence, in turn, results in a purposeful reach toward the sky. He alternates his hands as he speaks the first three phrases, hand dropping into a fist, arm muscles further bulging in response. After stating the third need, he pauses, wiping sweat from his perfectly manicured brows. Then, lifting both hands in the air, he points straight at the camera and speaks the words *from you*, no sooner crossing his arms in defiance across his chest. The video would be even more hilarious if it weren't so true. Whether we're talking about the biggest Sunday morning of the church calendar year or just another day at church camp, the dramatics are real. The show must go on, or for our purposes here, the show must be *put* on—even if this is also, oftentimes, the best part of camp.

When kids go to camp, they expect everything about the whole week to be big. Whether it's a child's first summer or their ninth year in a row (and they sport an impressive collection of camp T-shirts to prove it), campers are often blown away by the theatrics of seven days at church camp. Where else can they gorge from a communal hundred-foot-long trough filled with ice cream, chocolate syrup, and whipped cream? Where else does music accompany their every step from early wake-up calls to slumbering lights-out lullabies to three-hundred-person choruses sung before a roaring campfire? Where else do women dressed in red, white, and blue sequined spandex zip line through the dining hall during a meal, all for the sake of breaking down walls and making someone laugh?

Memories like these oftentimes only happen at camp when staff are encouraged not only to think big but to be big too. Campers, in turn, can't help but buy into an environment of excess. Camp, after all, is campy. It leans into an identity of being big and outlandish, of absurd exaggeration and ridiculous hilariousness, and rightfully so: all of this is what makes camp *camp*. Even those who are critical of camps—like Susan Sontag, essayist behind "*Notes on 'Camp,'*" who defined its key elements as "artifice frivolity, naïve middle-class pretentiousness, and shocking excess"[4]—recognize that campy excesses are often what draw campers in the first place and keep them coming back for more.

For Kristin Wolven, a former program director at Mission Spring's Frontier Ranch, camp was critical to her later career as a reality television producer. "I loved being on the program team," she told me in an interview. Her eyes sparkled at the memory, a faint chuckle erupting from her mouth. "Camp is where I learned how to produce. It's where I learned how to organize people on a stage to tell a bigger story. On shooting day, prior to filming, I would gather the contestants and go over the challenge for the episode: the rules, the details, the timeline. Then the cameras would roll, and I'd let them loose."

Desperate as I was to probe further into the fabrication of reality television shows, I later found myself wondering if Kristin ever reconciled the performance aspect of her experience at camp. Did she ever feel like she was selling Jesus to hundreds of campers every week too? Did putting on a show every week feel a little off to her, as if the whole of the Christian faith had to be made bright and shiny in order to sell the spiritual goods? She and I didn't get to those questions, at least not that day; instead, we stuck to the script and to the questions I had sent over to her beforehand.

In reality, the impact of being on camp staff was profound: more than twenty years later, she credits much of her spiritual journey to the four summers she spent in Scotts Valley, California. But there were also doctrinal truths about the Christian faith Kristin had to unlearn, truths she is still unlearning today. She had to unlearn the labeling often found in white evangelicalism—a black-and-white way of thinking that often adheres to only one way of seeing the world. This was true when it came to Christian concepts like sin, heaven, hell, God's will, and prayer, but also to *people* the Christian church often labeled as deserving of perceived places like heaven and hell because of the supposed sin in their lives. More than two decades later, Kristin wasn't afraid to voice her doubts; she wasn't afraid to hold the tension of a place that proved incredibly formative to her personhood, even if she questioned whether winning souls for Jesus was the most important thing.

When she raised a question about the prescribed camping model for the second time in our conversation, I couldn't help but laugh: "Should a bunch of twenty-year-olds be leading three hundred kids to Christ when their prefrontal cortex is not fully developed?" As young, twenty-something seasonal summer staff employees, we, too, acted as converters. More often than not, our job was to win over and change, to turn around and bend and transform. In this environment, conversion was the end goal, the ultimate objective, the entire point. Conversion meant we were doing it right, even if we were just doing what we were told, following in the legacies of those who had gone before us.

I suppose Kristin's story is part of my story too. I may not have been leading future reality television stars down pathways to stardom, but I did learn how to put on a show for the many campers who crossed over pathways to camp—all in the name of Jesus and for purposes of conversion *to* Jesus. And put on a show, I did.

I squirted chocolate syrup over unholy amounts of ice cream in hundred-foot-long troughs that were eventually filled with regurgitated spit. I sang songs, led songs, practiced songs, and taught others the words and motions to songs like "Look All Around You," "For I Am Persuaded," and "Somebody's Calling Out Your Name." It is entirely possible that every lyric and hand motion, courtesy of camp songs from 1988 through 2014 or so, live eternally in the recesses of my mind. I rode zip lines forty feet above the ground in Americana-colored spandex while "American Woman" by Lenny Kravitz played on loudspeakers in the background.[5] (It should also be said that I carried a watermelon while riding said zip line, not in an effort to imitate Baby from *Dirty Dancing* but to honor the Fourth of the July. If fire permits don't allow for a display of fireworks, one can at least watch fruit explode from on high and call it *fruit* works.) As I recall these memories, I can only smile: there's nothing like a week at church camp, that much is true.

But sometimes putting on a show for Jesus crosses a line. When the programmatics of church camp move from the precepts of loving God and loving other people in places of pristine nature to instead selling the theatrics of a major world religion in a manicured luxury resort, we've somehow gotten it wrong. God isn't something to be sold, even if we humans thought that was part of the deal.

If we could break down walls, then we could gain their trust. And if we could gain their trust, then we could convince them of our beliefs—of an individualistic kind of saving that only happens at the hands of a man named Jesus. Because if we could just do this, then everything would be okay in the end. This became our story because it was the tale passed down to us, a narrative that came from a place of tradition and belief and from the very foundations on which white evangelicalism and the Christian camping movement were built.

/ / /

Evangelicalism traces its roots back to the Methodist revival that took place in Great Britain in the 1700s, when a belief about the universal love of God birthed the entire Methodist denomination. Revivals kept on happening all across Europe: The people loved Jesus! The Europeans awoke to God! Eventually, whether through a homing seagull or a giant cousin of the *Mayflower*, a similar message made its way across the pond to North America. The Great Awakening, as it came to be called, was big on conversion experiences. Instead of a reliance on the sacraments and traditions, Scripture and missionary work took the helm. In the States, this spiritual wake-up call was marked by men like Jonathan Edwards, John and Charles Wesley, and George Whitefield. A century later, the Second Great Awakening led to a period some historians have called the "Evangelical Empire"[6]: large swaths of evangelicals dominated cultural institutions like schools and universities, involving themselves in the temperance movement and supporting various causes, such as the abolition of slavery, as well as education and criminal reform.

Around this same period, organized youth camping saw its origins in the Northeast: The rise of industrialization and urbanization birthed back-to-nature and "fresh air" camps, as well as various youth movements, camp meetings, and compulsory education. From the Salvation Army to the Jewish Working Girls Vacation Society, many of the camps were religiously motivated, combining "outdoor spiritual enrichment with a respite from city life."[7] The advent of two more definitive religious movements, the camp meeting and the religious conference, subsequently birthed a bouncing tot called early American religious camps.

Now, picture this part of the story for a second: Americans were moving westward, caravans of covered wagons dotting landscapes across the Midwest, over the Rockies, and onward toward states like Oregon, Washington, and California. Largely communal, people gathered outdoors, sharing meals and telling stories of life along the way. An avid camper myself, although I have not crossed unchartered terrain in a covered wagon, I have spent a fair number of nights under the stars. Warm embers of the campfire easily become a mesmerizing light, magically giving way to conversations that can't seem to happen anywhere else. It's not hard to imagine how the same may have happened for the early settlers when, at the end of a long day's journey, campfires on prairies and plains brought forth a unique kind of storytelling we call *camp meetings* today.

According to historians at the ACA (American Camp Association), the singular purpose of these meetings was conversion: "The structure of the camp meeting moved participants toward commitment to Jesus Christ. Singing, exhortations, testimonials, and preaching were elements of small and large meetings. Often the camp meeting closed with a love feast, a symbolic shared meal in which all new converts participated."[8] From the origins of camp meetings and early organized youth camping initiatives, religious conferences eventually entered the scene, with a focus on the whole of the church rather than on personal salvation. It wasn't until the late 1930s, when children began attending family conferences in large numbers, that the "International Council of Religious Education became concerned about the inappropriateness of the Bible conference model for children under twelve."[9] As a result, religious camps and conference centers began to chase after decentralized models of church camping and instead sought to emphasize small group interactions.[10]

Just as camping ministries deepened into versions more closely aligned to what we see today, camping began to branch secularly and ecumenically, including into what we now call *evangelicalism*. "After World War II, a new generation of conservative Protestants rejected the separatist stance of fundamentalism and began calling themselves evangelicals,"[11] writes public historian Matthew A. McIntosh. Evangelicalism became marked by celebrity preachers like Billy Sunday, Aimee Semple McPherson, and Billy Graham, who "joined a tradition of charismatic men who preached an individualistic gospel, used mass media to amplify their message, and aligned themselves with mainstream celebrities to lend cultural credence to their message."[12] Evangelicals themselves also became known by a single denominator: an admiration for Graham himself.

Likewise, celebrity crossovers like singer Pat Boone and Stuart Hamblen, the hard-drinking "cowboy singer,"[13] thrived among this new brand of Jesus followers, and a number of evangelical institutions, such as the National Association of Evangelicals, *Christianity Today* magazine, and various educational institutions, began their origin stories. From this generation came droves of evangelical parachurch organizations, including Youth for Christ, Young Life, CRU, InterVarsity Christian Fellowship, and the Navigators. Flourishing outside of traditional denominational structures, some of these "evangelical groups, most notably Young Life, identified the summer camp model as fertile ground for conversion and religious experience."[14]

Not unlike the growth of evangelicalism in pulpits across America, by the 1960s, evangelical summer camps further divided the youth camping scene: as Mainline camps shifted away from "conversion toward character building, a new generation of Evangelical camps was mobilized."[15] It was in these very church camps that I found a home, a place to belong, and a people to call my own for nearly two decades of my teenage and adult life. Here, camp was "recognized as an 'effective delivery system' of the gospel message,"[16] and with conversion stories publicized far and wide, this part of the Christian camping scene quickly grew. Jacob Sorenson, a practical theologian and camping enthusiast, states that by the 1970s, Young Life camps alone served nearly 17,000 young people each summer (a number that has since grown to over 250,000). With a "camp model focused on small groups and relationship building . . . other mid-century Evangelical camps featured large group rallies, emotional altar calls, and dynamic preachers."[17] This, of course, is just one example of a conversion-based camping model. While certain aspects of the model differed, one thing became true in evangelical camping that remains true today: they yearned to see each and every camper be won to Christ through a deeply personal, religious experience.

There's an additional leap that happens in this story, though, and that's a leap into the wild waters of *white* evangelicalism specifically. But defining white evangelicalism isn't as simple as saying: white people + evangelical Christianity = white evangelicalism. Too often, the identifiers of white evangelicals themselves prove harder to solve than a third-grade math problem. The definition exists in understanding the defining attributes of *belief* that subsequently mark a *people*. After all, "white evangelical camping" is not a known association: instead, if camps display characteristics commonly associated with religious, cultural, and political preferences that align with evangelical Christianity, *then* they might just be classified as a white evangelical church camp.

Theologically, "evangelicals are people who take the Bible really seriously . . . (or at least some carefully selected parts of it)," as a writer from Religion News Service quips.[18] For years, evangelicals were simply defined by the Bebbington quadrilateral: the Bible, the cross, the concept of being born again, and activism. Some say evangelicals are people who check "born-again Christian" on the religious preferences section of an online dating profile, while others are those who make up the 81 percent who voted for former president Donald J. Trump in the 2016 election. When it comes to politics, the majority of these folks vehemently oppose abortion and enthusiastically hold their signs high for traditional definitions of marriage—that marriage is only supposed to be between a man and a woman, so bakers in Colorado should reserve the right to not have to decorate a cake for a same-sex couple.

But in *Reading Evangelicals*, historian Daniel Silliman defines "white evangelicals by the novels they have made bestsellers in the last four decades."[19] For Silliman, an editor at *Christianity Today* magazine, when it comes to white evangelicals, the old adage "you are what you read" is truer than ever before. *Love Comes Softly* and *This Present Darkness* uplifted the suburbs and gave rise to the culture wars; the *Left Behind* series gave voice to a theme of "individual choice, as the characters have to confront the total implausibility of what is happening around them and make a conscious decision to believe the Rapture is true in every respect."[20] Finally, an Amish "bonnet thriller" called *The Shunning* and a book named *The Shack* twisted evangelical panties in a bunch when a Black woman God and a sprightly female Holy solidified further questions of authenticity and individualism.[21]

As intriguing as Silliman's argument is, I notice he doesn't always pair *white* and *evangelical* together. Sometimes, the latter stands alone. It's not until he and I grab a couple of minutes on the phone that an answer arrives: white evangelicalism is entirely about particular conversations at hand.

Because evangelicalism itself is not a church, a denomination, or even an ascribed theology, anyone can flow in and out of the conversation. A variety of people can flow in and out of any given conversation the gatekeepers deem matters; others, in turn, are also defined by whether or not they're a part of that conversation and by their marked participation *in* the conversation. In Silliman's book, bookstores became the carriers of cultural and theological conversations when specific themes found in a handful of bestselling books encompassed an entire group of people. It's not, then, that white evangelicals even have to identify as *white* (or even as evangelical, for that matter) but that the conversations that characterize this particular group of people and the belief system that follows largely center, benefit, and advance those who are white. In this way, white evangelicalism becomes a matter of inclusion and exclusion; it becomes a structural story of space and tradition, of those who play a role in the greater conversation and those who do not.

We may not have been reading *The Shack* as a camp summer staff crew, but we lived by the themes present in Silliman's assertion. Although it's impossible to know exactly how many children and youth from the suburbs attend church camps, we do know that "suburban families in particular have prioritized sending their children to camps in order to give them a respite from their often hectic lives."[22] Take, then, the opinion regarding the rise of culture wars: we also may not have been training campers to rally for an end to abortion (as documentary filmmakers eerily predicted in the 2006 film *Jesus Camp),* but when "white American evangelicals took the activist playbook from the very Civil Rights leaders they opposed" in order "to advance a moral agenda they could support,"[23] culture wars naturally found an inroad into white evangelical camping culture. Think about the typical seven-day talk sequence: the point was to preach the gospel, or, as evangelical superstar Jerry Falwell asserted, to "preach the word." The point, as we well know by now, was conversion. But the point was an introduction into theological interpretations a great majority of white evangelicals hold in order to "reject calls for social justice by invoking the gospel of Jesus Christ."[24] To Jared Stacy, an American pastor and PhD candidate in theological ethics, when this rejection happened, "evangelicals ignored their participation in development and direction of America's social and moral establishment. They had no qualms about working for culture change along different moral lines post-Civil Rights."[25] When camp speakers, such as myself, followed directions to piously, simply *preach the gospel,* this was not a matter of giving up power but was instead a "projection of [our] power and authority."[26] What is most important? Preaching the gospel—which is to say, telling people that what we believed was the only right way when it came to what they should believe and, ultimately, how they should live. To what would white evangelicals not hand over space? Issues of racial and social justice. In turn, marginalized communities that already lacked power within the space continued to remain adversely affected. As Stacy reminds his reader, "Culture War Christianity shows its power in its speaking and its silence."[27]

The final three books Silliman offers his reader all celebrate common themes of individualism and authenticity. From the stage and from the second sports field to the right of the dining hall, we rolled out a red carpet of applause when it came to an individual's right to live an authentic life as God intended for them to do. Say a special prayer and ask Jesus into your heart so he can become Lord and Savior of your life? Let the good times roll (even if the conception of such a prayer isn't located anywhere in the New Testament or the Bible as a whole). Conquer a relay race called Bizerko in record time by drinking a cupful of slop left over from the previous meal? We celebrate the vomit that will most certainly stream forth from your mouth and crown you victor of all, young camper.[28]

Likewise, to Kristin Du Mez, historian and author of *Jesus and John Wayne*, the white evangelical movement was solidified with men like John Wayne and Ronald Reagan. Not only did these men embody the ideals that would come to mark white evangelicalism, but they were also "instrumental in whipping up anti-communist sentiment in the

US, building credibility with a religion focused on individualism."[29] As much as individualism is celebrated in American culture, it is perhaps even more celebrated within certain religious cultures, including at white evangelical church camps. I can't tell you how many times I stood in front of a group of middle school students and leveraged the *choice* they had when it came to matters of faith. I often said something like this: "You may not be able to choose where you go to school or who your parents are. You don't even sometimes get to choose your friends. But you do get to choose whether or not you say yes to God's invitation. You do get the choice as to whether or not you want to follow Jesus with your whole heart. The choice is up to you."

Evangelicalism, after all, is a matter of personal preference and choice. Katelyn Beaty, author of *Celebrities for Jesus*, writes that evangelicals are often marked by an "individual conversion experience and to verbally share the faith with others. In this formula, individuals have a powerful experience with Christ that they try to inspire in other individuals . . . the first order of things was individuals coming to Christ, prompted by the preaching of a dynamic individual figure."[30] From this choice to follow Jesus, everything else follows—and everything else is celebrated. The rugged individualism celebrated in American culture becomes further exemplified and lifted up as the ultimate message and end goal: *You* pull yourself up by your bootstraps. *You* work hard so you can own the house and buy all the things and go on all the vacations. This is what it means to live the American dream because this is what it means to buy into this particular brand of culture. *You* get to do it all, thanks to Jesus Christ, who did it all on his own too. Eleven-year-old church camp attendees may not be envisioning a future house in the suburbs with a dog and 2.5 children to boot when they say a special prayer and ask Jesus into their hearts, but the invitation *to* choose has profound consequences on the life that follows. A singular picture of what it means to follow Jesus becomes the very definition of being a Christian.

In more ways than one, authentic engagement means accepting an invitation into conformity, which is to say, into an idealized image of Jesus followers. Conversion into white evangelicalism means buying into the "myth of rugged individualism, family values, and traditional gender roles as a response to the cultural uprisings linked to communism, women's liberation, and the Civil Rights Movement"[31]—even if this understanding is never stated from the front of the room or isn't realized for another twenty years, if ever.

Sometimes it feels like the weight of conversion is something I'm just beginning to wrap my mind around, just beginning to understand. A conversation with a friend I've known for nearly twenty years helped me begin to put the pieces of the puzzle together.

Jackson Stone, a former camp musician and program director, was raised in the Southern Baptist tradition but quickly found a home, and a calling, in the parachurch outreach organization Young Life. He became involved with the group as a seventh grader and by the end of his eighth-grade year had made up his mind to become a camp musician. By nineteen, his dream had become a reality when he landed a spot as a camp musician at a national camp.

"It just snowballed from there," Jackson recalled when the two of us were able to grab a few minutes on the phone. For Jackson, a white man, the privilege baked into his experience is undeniable: he knew the right people. An extrovert to the core, he is a connector and a networker. If he says he's going to call you, he'll call you; if he thinks you should connect with his buddy Alec from the deep woods of Arkansas, you're going to connect with Alec from the deep woods of Arkansas and learn all about the Boggy Creek Monster, underground caverns, and the continued impact of desegregation at Little Rock High School. These traits, combined with natural, gifted musical sensibilities, quickly helped Jackson rise up the ranks within the organization. Make no mistake: Jackson is grateful for his time in Young Life and for the many ways it helped him grow. For a long time (and certainly in the early years), his theology was congruent with the organization's mission to introduce young people to Jesus. But as his theology evolved, he began to question their approach.

But by the time Jackson was in his midthirties, he started to push back against some of Young Life's core policies, namely around LGBTQ+ inclusion. When a volunteer youth leader approached him about inviting one of her friends, who was gay, to become a volunteer, Jackson gave what he later described as a canned response: *It's against policy. It'd be a risk to our students to have a same-sex-attracted person serving in leadership. They're welcome to attend events, but they can't serve in leadership.* By the time he got home that night, he could only describe the previous interaction as gross and inauthentic, like he'd become a real company man. But the conversation sparked something else in him: it led him to understand why and how he'd been wrong in a number of different areas. Eventually, it guided him toward new understandings, including in his beliefs about conversion.

"A major objective of camp is conversion," Jackson finally said. "I knew exactly what I was doing because I bought into the model of this particular spiritual mission. There's a lot of people who don't understand that part of the camping model: we wanted campers to convert to Christianity and believe the way we believed, to make them more like us. We did this instead of simply loving young people, no strings attached." Listening to Jackson almost felt like an out-of-body experience: I could feel my fingers typing furiously, but I could also hear affirmative *mmms* and *hmms* coming from my mouth. His experience put words to something I had only just begun to process.

"When I look back on it now, I can't help but see threads of manipulation and coercion. I didn't think so at the time, but I can believe it now. My mission in life was to introduce kids to Jesus and have them believe in a certain way." Jackson paused. Silence squeaked its way into our conversation. Even though nearly a decade had passed since he took the stage at camp, the memories of his time at Young Life camps don't feel so far away. As a musician, he purposefully chose songs that would draw campers in, "that took them from the heights of fun and excitement down to a place of certain belief." Every element on stage was purposeful and exact, pointing to an end goal of conversion.

Jackson, who left the evangelical tradition, became ordained in the United Methodist Church, and now serves as a chaplain in the military, mourns the loss of community that once accompanied the church camp world. But he also embraces what he describes as a deeper, better journey of theological evolution—including an evolution of his understanding of conversion. When Jackson really began to study the person of Jesus, he saw that Jesus wasn't trying to get people to convert to another religion: he was just trying to get them to change their minds, to repent, to look for a better way to live.

My conversation with Jackson makes me think about my own spiritual journey: I, too, have walked away from evangelicalism. Just as I mourn the loss of relationships that felt cemented through shared experience, mission, and expressions of belief, I think about the role I played in conversion. Like Jackson, I was a converter; every word that came out of my mouth had an aim to win over and change, to turn around and bend and transform.

Because I believed conversion was essential to the Christian faith, I didn't see anything *wrong* with this role. That's what I was supposed to do, what *we* were supposed to do. It was just part of the gig. But something happened along the way: the last thing I wanted to do was try to sell Jesus, let alone feel like I was being sold a version of Jesus. In the end, I didn't want to be a mouthpiece for a gospel that required me to make a commodity of faith too small to shine on its own.

/ / /

I return to a game of hide-and-go-seek, which is to say, to a couple of questions of readiness. *Are you ready ("Ready!") for the week ahead? Are you ready ("Ready!") to have the best week of your life? Are you ready ("Ready!") to be found?* Being found, in this sense, meant drinking the Kool-Aid of conversion. Being found sometimes meant making God into a transactional product to be bought and sold—or maybe, even more specifically, into something that needed to be *advertised* to allow for purchase further down the road. While the critics among us (that I imagine identify as evangelical, who view conversion as an essential stakeholder of the Christian faith) may bristle at this interpretation, I don't think the idea is too far from the truth.

As Jackson so aptly reminded me, Jesus wasn't actually in the business of winning souls. He wasn't actually trying to get people to convert to another religion; he was just trying to get them to change direction. He wasn't about making the gospel (which is to say, himself) relevant and attractive as to keep the campers coming back year after year, nor was he about gimmicks and giveaways, hipsters and happy hours.[32] I imagine Jesus would have shuddered at the phrase "It's a sin to bore a kid with the gospel," words I touted the virtues of for years as a truncated version of a quote originally attributed to Jim Rayburn, the founder of Young Life. The organization has continued to both abbreviate and celebrate Rayburn's original words, most notably at its camps: "We believe it is sinful to bore kids with the gospel. Christ is the strongest, grandest, most attractive personality to ever grace the earth. But a careless messenger with the wrong method can reduce all this magnificence to the level of boredom . . . it is a crime to bore anyone with the gospel."[33] To declare lack of entertainment a sin is a misnomer in and of itself. To say that boredom is a crime or that the Christ cannot be strong and grand and attractive on his own accord, without the help of anyone else, is wholly inaccurate. To believe that children and youth—or humans, in general—lack the intellectual capacity to discover God without the shiny assistance of a verbal messenger is altogether wrong. God needs not a display of flashing neon lights, wild theatrics, and curated music sets to be made known.

In truth, that dogmatic phrase plays on repeat like a broken record player in the back of my mind. Its declaration was something I believed could not be argued, especially when it came to the first night's talk. If my role was to break down walls and win over campers in order to eventually extend an invitation of conversion, then I had to tell the funniest stories. I had to be the most animated. I had to be the best "girl speaker" (or so some would call me) any camper had ever heard. I had to be the most likable, the most winsome, and the most down-to-earth person—which is to say, the strongest, grandest, most attractive personality to ever grace the likes of camp. I had to be a fleshier version of the Man I wanted campers to purchase by the end of the week—money back, guaranteed.

But if God is not a commodity to be bought and sold, then Christ the Great Liberator is already enough. Then the mountains and the hills, the trails and the skies of all these sacred playgrounds are already enough. Then inviting children and youth to simply show up and be changed by a place where God and nature meet is already enough. Camp staff, we're off the hook! There's nothing we have to do to actually *get* the wheels in motion because *that* God and *this* place already have it handled. We can just sit back and enjoy the ride because something *is* going to happen in that place, that week. But it's not because of anything we did or will do on our own parts because it's never actually *been* about anything we've ever done on our parts.

In more ways than one, the gears are already in motion for such a movement when campers show up to camp and are forced to unplug from technology for a week. In my research, numerous overnight camps, on both the secular and religious sides of the fence, are starting to tout and advertise the benefits of "getting unplugged" to prospective parents, caregivers, and youth group leaders. There is, no doubt, a benefit to immersing oneself in nature—and to both the young and the old—to getting away from screens and technology that are constantly, increasingly vying for one's attention.[34]

But mostly, church camp just doesn't need to try to sell God anymore. Disillusioned by a brand of Christianity that "sought to lure millennials back by focusing on style points: cooler bands, hipper worship, edgier programming, impressive technology,"[35] the late Rachel Held Evans eventually found a home in the Episcopal Church: "Every week I find myself, at age 33, kneeling next to a gray-haired lady to my left and a gay couple to my right as I confess my sins and recite the Lord's Prayer. No one's trying to sell me anything. No one's desperate trying to make the Gospel hip or relevant or cool. They're just joining me in proclaiming the great mystery of faith—that Christ has died, Christ has risen, and Christ will come again—which, in spite of my persistent doubts and knee-jerk cynicism, I still believe most days."[36] Whether a tiny Episcopal parish in the foothills of Dayton, Tennessee, an enormous church camp and conference center nestled in the valley of the San Bernardino Mountains, or a beloved Covenant camp perched on the waters of Lake Geneva, the same message applies: we need not try to sell Jesus to our constituents.

Instead, on the first night of camp, but then on every night that follows, we error on the side of welcome and embrace, "not simply to the religious and the privileged, but to the poor, the marginalized, the lonely and the left out."[37] This is all that matters, to every camper, to every kid. To all who enter, we offer the warmest of receptions. We give a question of readiness a whole new meaning.

2

God the Mostly Father

A story I told at church camp returns to me: I was four or five years old, my brother two years younger than me. All we wanted in life was to fulfill our dreams of becoming superheroes, so our mama, who knew her way around a sewing machine, decided to help us out. She sewed a Superman cape for my brother and a Strawberry Shortcake cape for me.

Lest the campers doubted the superpowers of the '80s relic Strawberry Shortcake, I told them how she fought the world with her super, strawberry-smelling strength. Often, turning around, my back to the audience, I showed them the very cape I'd sported as a young child: one large, champagne berry lay centered in the middle of stretchy rose-colored fabric. A slack elastic band, worn thin by use, itchily grabbed at the sides of my neck. Relic firmly in place, I told the story of a dare—of a time when Strawberry Shortcake dared Superman to do what Superman did best and fly, down a set of stairs no less. Years later, I find myself wondering if the story is mere exaggeration or an actual tale of family lore: when I ask my brother and, later, both of my parents to recall the memory, I get three different interpretations. Regardless of semantics, meaning is found in the aftermath of a two-year-old child who attempted the supernatural.

"When the younger brother accepts his wiser, older sister's dare to fly down the stairs," I dared the campers believe, "Strawberry Shortcake begins a dramatic countdown: *three . . . two . . . one . . . go!* There is a palpable pause before an inevitable *thump, thump, thump* ensues down a carpeted set of stairs in a little brown house in Tillamook, Oregon. Superman does not actually fly, as it turns out, for his magical red cape does not allow his mere toddler human self to defy the weaker planet's pull."

The mountain peak of the story drew closer by the second. When my father, who sat on the couch reading the newspaper (or perhaps watching the CBS Evening News), heard a *thump, thump, thump* coming from the general direction of the stairwell, his ears perked up. This was no ordinary sound, no regular thump. Bounding from the couch to the stairs in one swift motion, he sprinted through the house like an Olympian. Here, the storyteller in me came alive, my face contorting into bursts of animation, my entire body alive in the retelling. I let the scene slow, my voice mimicking a questionable version of the theme music from *Chariots of Fire* as my arms and legs pretended, in slow motion, to run toward the thumping sound. There on stage, I dropped to my knees, arms outstretched and hands cupped together toward the bottom step of an imaginary set of stairs.

My voice falling to a whisper, the next sentence tied it all together: "My father got there just in time—just in time to scoop his son up in his arms. Because that's what the Father does. The Father always scoops his children up in his love."

Point made, I probably paused for a second or two, both to catch my breath and to let the declaration sink in. I doubt I took off the Strawberry Shortcake cape as I continued to tell the story of a Father who desperately loved his children, including each and every one of the campers who sat before me.

/ / /

If Night One was a time of wild welcome (albeit encased in a determined, conversion-driven sales pitch), then Night Two rolled out the red carpet of the Christian religion. Here, God took center stage. In order to understand the narrative and move campers along a continuum of belief, a speaker had to start at the very beginning—starting with the one who is God. "Look at the sky, the trees, the water all around you," I probably said, more than once. "That's God the Creator. Think about the wonder, love, excitement you experienced in this place today: that's the God who loves you, the one we call *Father*." In such a role, I used every illustration at my disposal, not only to build my case but also to debunk any mistruths students may have picked up along the way. Here, a picture was worth a thousand words: be it by PowerPoint or a grainy set of enlarged photocopies, courtesy of the antiquated camp copy machine, a collection of images often told the story of God.

Sometimes the night started with an invitation for campers to select the correct image of God. Call it a game of Pick 'n' Choose, multiple choice, or a single question in a goofy edition of Trivial Pursuit, the selection of images often looked something like this:

- *Image #1: The Great Judge.* A white-wigged, peach-skinned judge sits behind a gnarled wooden desk, gavel in hand. Is God the Great Judge, a scowling, unapproachable magistrate who casts down decisions and rules his people from above?
- *Image #2: Santa Claus.* A laughing, merry, light-skinned man with a long white beard and mustache sits on a large red and gold throne. He is dressed in a red suit and stocking cap with white trim. His boots are black for tromping-through-snow purposes. A bounty of gifts lay at his feet, stacked up, one after another. Is God more like Santa Claus? He may not show up all that often, but he sure wants to make you happy with all those presents!

- *Image #3: Mr. Pie-in-the-Sky.* A smiling man with tanned golden skin and long, hippie-like hair relaxes in a Barcalounger,[1] twiddling his thumbs. He looks rather peaceful, like he just finished a morning surf sesh in balmy San Diego waves. He looks pretty cool, too, because this whole *idea* of a God like him is pretty cool: he created the world, after all, even if he is rather laidback and uninvolved now.
- *Image #4: The Loving Father.* A white man with clean-cut hair, a button-up shirt (because he just came from his white-collar job at the office), and a baseball cap (so he can easily transition to coaching his kid's little league baseball team) stands with his arms outstretched, ready for a hug. He is the father who loves you more than life itself, who shows up at every soccer game and piano recital alike, who wants the very best for you. This caring father only hopes you'll want to know him in return.

For years, I listened as one repeat camp speaker showed a handful of similar images to hundreds of campers seated before him. Wide-eyed, the children *ooh*ed and *aah*ed, casting votes for the correct answer. "Campers, raise your hand if you think God is the Great Judge!" A handful of hands would go up, the eyes of those who raised their hands wide with uncertainty once they realized the majority of campers hadn't picked that answer. The same went for answers 2 and 3, along with the inevitable "ho, ho, ho" shouted from deep within the bowels of the campfire pit when a picture of December's favorite fictional character graced the screen. When it came time to cast a vote for the fourth option, a majority of hands shot into the air. Of *course,* God was the caring, loving Father, the one who cheered the loudest at all your proverbial soccer games and piano recitals alike. Of *course,* God desperately wanted to know his beloved child, the God-created one he already loved with wild abandon. This storyline—of a loving Father who already loves you more than life itself—was exactly where a speaker wanted an audience to land early in the week, even if each *of course* felt more like the campers were just playing along, giving the answer they knew the grown-ups wanted to hear. Because if the big idea of God as a loving Father could be established on the second night of camp, then Jesus could be brought into the picture as his son on the third night of camp. With both of these elements clearly sealed in place, a case for what evangelicals historically call the Four Spiritual Laws easily gelled into place on the remaining nights of camp.

Boiled down to their gritty essence, one might say the Four Spiritual Laws go as follows: 1) God the Father loves you, and his son, Jesus, is a supercool dude. 2) Dirty rotten sinners can't know this love because all of humanity is tainted by sin. 3) Jesus saved the day by dying on the cross for you. 4) Believe in Jesus, and you can know God![2] Originally published as a religious tract by Bill Bright, the founder of Campus Crusade for Christ (now known as CRU) in the mid-'60s, the booklet outlined "his view of the essentials of the Christian faith concerning salvation."[3]

These essentials, along with a prayer of repentance or "turning" at the end of the brochure, are far-reaching: according to one report, the tract itself has been passed out to over 2.5 billion people worldwide.[4] Not only did Bright's beliefs become a stalwart of CRU, but a number of denominations and parachurch organizations such as the Billy Graham Evangelistic Association and Young Life also adopted his thoughts, "making the theology of Bill Bright (from the perspective of population influenced), the single most influential presentation of the Gospel in history."[5] Is it any wonder the Four Spiritual Laws eventually found a home at church camp, among roaring campfires and choruses sung under a canopy of stars?

Within this framework, humans have been born with an innate propensity toward darkness and a lethal amount of evil in their hearts. Everyone in the world is really, really bad—or, in Christian-speak, sinful or depraved. In this scenario, if you ascribe to a theology of human depravity, then you believe God's deep love for humanity must live alongside (a male) God's answer to the cost of sin: eternal punishment for all that really, really bad sin. Because also in this scenario, the only solution is to accept Jesus Christ as your Lord and Savior—then you can get back to being with God. Why choose eternal punishment when a simple prayer can yield eternal joy and jubilee? In a pithy game of Pick 'n' Choose, who wouldn't pick option 4, the Loving Father, when this is the only version of God that checks all the right boxes and plays by the correct set of rules?

I think about my sixteen, my twenty-one, my thirty-year-old selves: at all these ages, in the many white evangelical camps I called home, I took the most famous of if-then statements, the one passed down from Bill Bright to the far reaches of church camps to me. I swallowed it hook, line, and sinker. Then I passed along the truths passed down to me—because, once again, in this scenario, if you believe in a theology of eternal torment, then just as God's action of sending Jesus was the kindest and most loving action a God could do, then sharing with other people the key to saving their inherently wretched souls was also the kindest and most loving action a believer could do in return.

Before the specifics of such a theology could come into play, though, I had to paint a picture of the Loving Father—this singular image the sun, moon, and stars on which everything hung. Without it, everything else crumbled.

/ / /

As a speaker, when I told the story of my father bounding in to "scoop up his son in love," a picture of my white father and our (white) family of origin often accompanied the story. I reasoned that a photograph like this helped campers connect the dots between my words and the greater message being told: of a Father who loved his children more than anything else, who bounded across proverbial living rooms to rescue his *thump, thump, thump* of a falling son. This idea is great in theory, but God is not white, and God is not male—and God, as it goes, is bigger than any singular image might capture. Because when the only image of God campers see is a white, male fatherly figure, then those who aren't white and male (and who won't, assumedly, ever see themselves as a father) can't see God in themselves, nor can they see how they might ever come to be made in this God's image. They don't fit the mold. They can't ever find an ultimate place of belonging because the image of a white man whose sperm may have fathered a child too easily evokes memories of exclusion, abandonment, and abuse of power, to name a few.

I think about a recent conversation with my friend Tiffany. She and I regularly send walkie-talkie messages to one another in the carpool drop-off line and on walks around the block with the dog. In one breath, we talk about Value Village runs and the importance of soft pants and the dreams we hold for ourselves and one another, sometimes deep down inside. We don't hold back, but we try our hardest to push one another toward the God who is equal parts heart-grabber and soul-tugger, even if the God we see now is not the same God we saw in our youth.

When the two of us lined up an official interview time together, I sent her a list of scripted questions to sit with before the scheduled hour: *What was the theology communicated or that you perceived at church camp? Are there specific truths about the Christian faith you had to unlearn as you got older? True or false: church camp was made for white, straight, evangelical kids. Why or why not?* As a former camper raised in the charismatic Assemblies of God tradition, I wanted to hear about her experiences and compare them with my own, perhaps more stoic versions of Christian spirituality. More than anything, though, I yearned to listen to Tiffany's perspective as an adoptee and as a woman of color.

When we met, I noticed the deep breaths she took before answering a question. Her eyes widen, and then they close; she chews and thinks over her words in a way that almost feels foreign to me.

"It goes something like this: As an adoptee and as a longtime church camp attendee, the storyline lacked imagination for anyone in my shoes," she finally said. I nodded my approval. I desperately wanted to hear more. "So when it comes to the whole Father-Son narrative, it left out anyone who felt like leftovers, whose fathers didn't want them, or whose personal experience didn't fit into this story. There was no imagination for acceptance in the storyline for somebody like me."

For Tiffany, who attended AG (Assemblies of God) camps in Washington state from the fifth grade through high school, the dissonance she experienced was real: camp was a place of constant love and affection. Her leaders loved and cared for her well, to the point that "they made me feel wholly lovable," she recalled. But as someone who has not met her birth father (and will likely never meet him either), Tiffany now sees the damage instilled in campers who also had never met or didn't know their own fathers. She thinks about those campers who had complicated relationships to their fathers. Hers was not a family "God would ordain," as she recalls camp leadership saying, of both her first *and* her second families. In this scenario, adoption *into* the family of

God became a terribly spiritualized ordeal: *adoption* was the only word used to describe acceptance into Christian belief systems (in that campers were adopted *from* sin). But it was a very piss-poor comparison with modern adoption.

"You're essentially saying my first family is bad," Tiffany explained. Our conversation reminds her of the younger girls who later came with her to camp when she was an eighteen-year-old mentor: all of them, herself included, came from a very poor, rural community, with lots of single moms, poverty, and meth. If campers—or staff members, for that matter—couldn't get on board with the concept of God as Father, then you just didn't get it, and you just didn't get *in*. Nearly twenty years later, Tiffany summed it up in a single statement: "If you couldn't get on board with the patriarchy, you didn't have a place in this orbit."

I can't shake her words: when it comes to camp, the place of my greatest belonging became a place relegated to scrapbooks and forgotten Facebook groups, to songs that pop into my memory at the most random of times and former campers who message my inbox when I least expect it. In all of these places, I am, as Madeleine L'Engle once said, "still every age that I have been. Because I was once a child, I am always a child. Because I was once a searching adolescent, given to moods and ecstasies, these are still part of me, and always will be."[6] When it comes to Tiffany's words, I wonder about the effects of patriarchal language and theology—of words and beliefs I gulped down like air because I thought it was the best way to connect with God, the *only* way that God could love me. My grown-up self can resist a system controlled by men that seeks to put women in secondary positions of power, but I cannot ignore the child and the adolescent and the young adult within me who came to know God through the image of a good Father. Can all these many versions of myself make space for each other? Can God still be found in the image of a caring dad, or is that something I also need to leave behind?

A conversation with another friend, Caz, comes to mind. A New Zealander, Caz grew up attending a Christian camp in the home of Middle-earth through an organization that helped the families of widowed, single mothers.[7] Having lost her father at a young age, she remembers hearing that God does everything for a reason, so she should be grateful for the many father figures God had provided her along the way. But the answers didn't change as Caz got older. Instead,

> No one held my questions with me; [they] just gave me answers. I distinctly remember one day someone talking about how we know and experience God's love by thinking about how our dads love us. And I remember thinking, Well, if that's true, then I can never know God's love. That same week of camp, I sang the song "Blessed Be the Name of the Lord." I got to the part you sing on repeat, *He gives and takes away, he gives and takes away,* and I remember thinking how terrible God was to take away my dad. But I also remember thinking that I could not

think that or say that, or I would be rejected by all those doting adults.

As a spiritual director and the executive director of The Simple Way, a community-based nonprofit organization in the Kensington neighborhood of Philadelphia, Pennsylvania, Caz has let go of a number of the ideas instilled within her at camp—including the belief that God is exclusively male or that she can only know God's love through knowing the love of a father. But she also no longer believes in the words she sang on repeat, in a God that gives and takes away. "God does not want little kids growing up without parents, feeling abandoned and sad, you know?" I could only nod my head in response.

Later that afternoon, I went down a rabbit trail of camp memories. Having stumbled on a moving box tucked away in the far reaches of the garage, I unearthed a collection of scrapbooks from the height of my camp days. Dozens of printed photos—some whole, others cut out around faces and bodies—adorned the pages. I was generous in my use of stickers and even more lavish with my words: nicknames, anecdotes, and song lyrics filled every inch of blank space. *I never want to forget, I never will forget,* I wrote next to one photograph. My face is smooshed alongside eleven other staff members I vowed to never forget. In truth, I have forgotten: I've forgotten how easily I believed, how much I wanted to believe, how much I wanted others to join me in this belief. A song we sang in rounds, voices filling the cobalt night sky, filled one corner of the page:

> *Father, I adore you,*
> *And I lay my life before you,*
> *How I love you.*

/ / /

We weren't wrong in our devotion, nor could our earnestness have been purer. But we were wrong in clinging to notions of God that could only be known through the love of a father, whom we believed a man and solely referred to as a male figure. The more we clung to this image, the more we upheld values of the *patriarchy*, a word writer Ashley Easter defines as a "social organization marked by the supremacy of the father in the clan or family, the legal dependence of wives and children, and the reckoning of descent and inheritance in the male line; broadly: control by men of a disproportionately large share of power."[8] At church camp, we made it easier for men to succeed than women: a man wasn't questioned about whether or not he could speak at camp. He wasn't told there were certain roles for which he lacked qualifications; instead, his penis single-handedly qualified him for anything he wanted to do.[9] But try to hand a woman a microphone, and her qualifications, her desire, and her entire identity will be questioned—not only because this goes against the norm of who an audience expects to see but also because it defies expectations of who a woman is expected to *be* at camp. One woman I interviewed was called *the devil's handmaiden* in one breath and a *Jezebel* in the next, simply because she was the first *female* camp speaker the white evangelical Christian camp had ever seen.[10] (Because this had also never been modeled to her, in the months before she was to speak, she went and purchased a pair of khaki pants and a button-down shirt, an outfit far from her usual attire. She bought into a belief that she had to be as masculine as possible to embody the role of camp speaker.) Another woman was invited to take a predominate leadership role on stage because "she's female, but she's funny"—as if the attribute of humor was finally enough to let her play in the big leagues. The number of times someone told me, "You're a really good girl speaker" is laughable, if this can even be a situation to which humor applies. I say this not to emphasize my ability to open my trap but to point out the doubtfulness of my male colleagues receiving a pat on the head for being "a really good boy speaker" after telling a story 'round the old campfire. *Good boy. Good boy, now sit!*

More often than not, in a church camp setting, men and women buy into complementarian beliefs of womanhood and manhood, believing that men and women have different but complementary roles and responsibilities in marriage, family life, and especially in religious leadership settings. In a way, the word *complementary* can sound rather innocuous, as if a woman is to a man what a tablespoon of peanut butter on one slice of bread is to a tablespoon of jelly on another slice of bread. Far from equal measures of beloved lunchtime sandwiches, the roles and responsibilities within a complementarian system are often hierarchical and connected to power dynamics. When a woman *is* actually given a seat at the table or offered a position of leadership, it doesn't come without consequence. She might question her place in the system, and then, because she is seen as an outlier by other women, she doesn't fit in anywhere else. She might try to mimic her male counterparts in words, actions, and, as we saw earlier, dress—not because she actually wants to speak or act or dress like a man but because *his* is considered the accepted norm, *her* most desirable goal.

Systems of the patriarchy rear their ugly heads in a thousand different ways in a church camp setting. Head to a camping website and count the number of (white) males in leadership positions. Do the same in a survey of major Christian camps that list upcoming speakers for each week of the summer. Many different facets of the patriarchy trickle down from there, but when it comes to cultural manifestations *of* male headship and female submission, there is no better illustration than purity culture.

The Purity Movement itself began in the 1990s by promoting a "strict view of abstinence before marriage, targeting adolescents, teens, and young adults with the message that they were either pure or impure/good or bad/Christian or non-Christian based on others' assessments of their sexual lives."[11] In line with traditional gender expectations, men were seen as "strong, 'masculine' leaders of the household, church, and (to a lesser extent) society," while women were their supportive right hand, raised to be "pretty, 'feminine,' sweet, supportive wives and mothers."[12] At camp, the movement explicitly played out around gendered sexual expectations, for both campers and staff. Here, a concept of purity reigned. Sexlessness for everyone, but especially for girls, became the expected and *accepted* norm. To no one's surprise, "girl campers" were generally considered the more *sexless* of the genders—sexual desire supposedly the least of a girl's worries. Young men were taught their minds were evil, whereas young women came to believe their bodies were evil—which is to say, "men's thoughts and actions are said to be either pure or impure, while women *themselves* are said to be either pure or impure."[13]

In my research, one interviewee remembers attending the "10 Reasons Why You Can't Have Sex before You're Married" seminar during a week at high school camp, while a former female staff member recalls the number-one question middle school campers asked during a sex talk breakout session: *How far is too far?* A number of women joked about the one-piece bathing suit rule, an absolute across Christendom so as not to make the men and boys "stumble."[14] Whether campers or staff members, the onus for young girls and women to protect their "brothers in Christ" lay entirely on them—because in this movement, it was the woman's *body* that caused the man's *mind* to stray. And for a number of the women I interviewed, shame accompanied the perceived responsibility to uphold the values of purity culture.

At camp, sexual metaphors almost entirely directed toward the female body took up space: Linda Kay Klein, author of *Pure*, writes about how "a 'pure' woman is compared to a brand new shiny car, while an 'impure' one is compared to a used car that everyone around town has already driven and that isn't worth much anymore; a 'pure' woman is compared to a delicious hamburger just set down on the table, while an 'impure' woman is compared to the last slobbery bite of that hamburger."[15] In another example, one interviewee remembers rose petals being ripped off a rose: the speaker would stand on the stage, an unblemished, virginal rose in his hands. *Who wants this rose?* he'd ask, leaning down and passing it around to some of the youth. He'd then take a petal or two off and then ask the next person to do the same. Eventually, the tarnished, crumpled rose was compared with a camper's purity: each hand it passed through symbolized yet another sexual partner and, perhaps even worse, yet another piece of a camper's heart. *Who wants this rose now?* he'd ask one last time. Whether or not he specifically called out girl campers didn't matter, not when women have historically been compared with roses, and the rose itself has stood for a female's reproductive organs. "Women are as roses, whose fair flower, being once displaced, doth fall that very hour," Shakespeare wrote in *Twelfth Night*.[16] We may not have uttered lines from the Bard at camp, but the meaning—and its intended audience—was clear.

Here's another example: in the play *Broken Heart*,[17] which has been performed for millions of high school students primarily at Young Life camps over the last forty years, a young girl finds solace through the figure of Jesus. When "Sally's" life begins to fall apart after her parents announce their divorce, Jesus, dressed in a white T-shirt, white jeans, and white sneakers (and often played by a white college-aged student), shows up. Meanwhile, Sally carries an orange, symbolizing her heart, with her wherever she goes on stage. Satan also comes onto the scene (dressed in black with hints of fiery red) and offers a collection of toys—a giant branch called the Twig of Bitterness, "which you can use to protect your heart," and a long, ten-inch nail called the Nail of Anger, so "if someone tries to hurt you, you can wound them with it."[18] The devil also gives Sally two more long nails called Jealously and Illicit Sex. Even though five-year-old Sally doesn't know what the heck Illicit Sex is, Satan promises high school Sally will know just what it is and how to use it when it's time.

A decade later, high school Sally has her "first real romance." But her decision to sleep with her boyfriend becomes a quick ticket to hell: emotion-heightening music plays in the background as Sally repeatedly stabs the orange with the elongated nail. When it's the boyfriend's turn to stab the orange, he rips through the flesh and leaves it mangled. By the time an inevitable breakup happens and Sally finally wonders aloud if God exists and, more importantly, if this God knows *she* exists, Jesus enters center stage. He takes her collection of tools, including Illicit Sex (which she now simply calls the Nail of Shame), and says, "These things you call toys, they are what nailed me to the cross."[19] She hands him the thorn branch, where her "heart" now rests, wrapped in protective aluminum foil; in a final moment of transformation, when Jesus reaches into the thorns and proceeds to unwrap the "armor" around her heart, the audience sees that the orange has suddenly been made whole. No longer used and mangled, Sally has been made pure again.

Although the play was written to introduce audiences to Jesus, its insinuations about women and expectations of the female body are obvious. In a blog post written nearly forty years after its creation, the playwright speaks of the emotional response teenagers had when the final music played: they began to cry, some silently, others loudly, a couple of them so overwhelmed by emotion that "they burst out the door to cry alone."[20] This came as no surprise to her because "Jesus wants us to give him the hurtful toys we use to cope with the pains of life, and he has the means to free us through what he suffered on the cross."[21] This comes as no surprise to me as well, having watched the play for the first time as a sophomore in high school. I, too, ran out of the room when the final scene commenced, tears streaming down my face. Feelings of sadness and heartache engulfed me, as well as a deep shame for the sex *I wasn't even having at the time* but would inevitably feel if I were ever to engage in any kind of "illicit sex."[22] Years later, I remembered the vows I made, vows to give my heart to Jesus and make responsible choices when it came to sex and drinking and drugs. Just like Sally, shame would creep in when I later, inevitably broke those same vows: I let down those to whom I had made vows. I let God down. I didn't play by the rules. So powerful was the metaphor of a ten-inch nail grinding into a pulpy piece of orange that when I find a copy of the play online and rewatch it from the comfort of my living room nearly three decades later, I don't know whether to shake my head in disbelief or weep for the power that purity culture held over me. The feelings become intimate once again, the anger and sadness and shame of my past a pounding, visceral reaction against my bones. It's like I still wear a key to purity around my neck, but I don't know the last time I actually thought about the girl who tried so hard to push the key into the lock.

Because wherever purity culture rears its supposedly innocent, blemish-free head, women are made to feel "responsible for the sexual thoughts, feelings, and choices men make, and so must dress, walk, and talk in just the right away so as not to 'inspire' sexual thoughts, feelings, and actions in them."[23] Several assumptions tend to accompany these teachings, mainly that gender is binary and that heterosexuality is the only "right" and "normal" kind of desire. This doesn't surprise me in the least, not when church camp continues to teach that girls are pink and boys are blue—and camp isn't the place to make purple, campers![24] As one interviewee who identifies as nonbinary noted, instructions to not make *dark* pink or blue were never any part of stated camp rules.

But culture now reveals more about how the movement is "based in nationalistic and white supremacist assumptions."[25] According to scholar and thought leader Bradley Onishi, the basic tenants of purity culture are only one step down from a "racialized and nationalistic view of marriage, sex, and the family."[26] In this world, if the teenage body can be disciplined into submission, then a foundation of a rightly ordered national body can be built. Decades later, it makes me wonder: was purity culture actually doing what it intended to do and disciplining my body into compliance?

To Onishi, the answer is clear as day, or at least as clear as the spray of a fire hose on Water Activities Day at church camp: "Purity culture is a projection of all the gendered, racial, and societal fears that white Christian nationalists harbor onto the canvas of teenage flesh."[27] For me and millions like me, we drank the water. We gulped down its truth, not knowing what actually lay underneath—not understanding how it would affect us and what it would do to our world in the days and years and decades to come.

/ / /

The story of Strawberry Shortcake in a superhero cape returns to me: Even though I've told the story a hundred times before, something comes alive within me. My heart beats wildly, fingers flying across the keyboard. I desperately believe in a God who loves with wild abandon, whose fleshy, amorphous arms scoop every last human up in love—this is what God is in the business of doing, over and over again. I can only believe in a God defined by love. The problem isn't in imagining God as a father scooping up a child in love; the problem arises when the image of God as a loving father becomes the *only* available image of God. If a camp speaker only uses illustrations that center Western notions of fatherhood and, subsequently, only refers to God by masculine pronouns, then it's easy for a child (or an adult, for that matter) to think of and picture and believe in a sole image of God as male.

"So is God male?" I asked Tiffany over the walkie-talkie app one day. "Do *you* still call God 'Father'?" I have my own answers to questions like these, but I wanted to hear her spell it out. Of the two of us, she's the one who runs in more conservative Christian circles, even if her own beliefs toe the line between progressive and more traditional versions of faith. She hems and haws; she probably spouts a line or two about soft pants before putting on her theological hat.

"The answer is simple," she finally said. "*God* is a verb, not a noun. Is God Father? Yes, as a verb. God is Father in action. God is Father in state, but God is not Father as a real, actual, fleshy noun of a man. God is not male." I pumped my fists in the air at Tiffany's words, or at least as much as I could while walking the dog and simultaneously holding a dog leash, a bag of poo, and a cell phone in my hands. God is neither male nor female but is instead revealed as being, Spirit, and imaged in both male and female.[28] But when God is only identified as male in church camp settings, then boys and girls—not to mention nonbinary children who identify as neither male nor female—can easily walk away with the belief that God is a bigger fan of boys than girls. Young children can also walk away with an understanding that God likes and uplifts and prefers men over women. For one professor, the equation is simple: "If God is like a male in relationship with the world who is like a female, and God is clearly superior to the world, then that image suggests that males are superior to females. When women are considered less like God, they cannot be fully human, because they cannot bear the *imago Dei* in the same way men do."[29] Of course, the reverse is true for men too: they can't be fully human if they're made to be like gods. But rejecting God's maleness is only the first step.

We must also reject the idea of God's whiteness. I think of social psychologist and author Christena Cleveland, who spent years speaking about racial reconciliation to congregations, justice organizations, and colleges within a mostly white evangelical world. Eventually, she felt she could no longer trust or believe in a white male God. As she writes in *God Is a Black Woman*, "For most of us, regardless of what we might *want* to believe or *claim* to believe, the image that immediately comes to mind when we imagine God is that of a powerful white man who is *for* and *with* powerful white men. It's a deceptive idea that flies under the radar, powerfully shaping us without our consent."[30] Embracing the Sacred Black Feminine and getting to know God as a Black woman was critical to Cleveland's future spirituality, as well as to her identity. A four-hundred-mile pilgrimage across the mountains of France brought her hope, healing, and liberation and gave her a renewed vision *of* God.

Mostly, though, it's the conversation with Tiffany that stays with me for a long time. Her words do something inside me: even if I would have given a similar answer had I been pressed, I needed to hear her say it aloud. I needed to hear it from someone who still dips her toes in evangelical-tinged waters of faith—from someone who still finds belonging in a place that still struggles to give women equal standing, that tends not to separate the idea of a male God from a male human being. I needed to hear I wasn't alone in my beliefs.

3

Superhero Jesus

By the third day of camp, things were getting good. Even though campers looked exhausted and ready to cozy up by the time they arrived at the campfire pit, clubroom, or evening meeting spot, the message was starting to ramp up. All the songs and skits and campy shenanigans took campers to a place of readiness to hear everything I had to say—including to the moment when the biggest superstar of all, Jesus himself, rode in on a proverbial shiny white horse.

"Friends, there is a God who loves you immensely," I would say. "And how he wants you to know his love for you! Two thousand years ago, he loved people just like us *so* much that he thought the greatest gift he could give them *then* and us *now,* and all the people in the future as well, was himself." At this point, I would often walk over to the side of the stage, to a giant box wrapped in shiny red wrapping paper and tied with an enormous white bow. Dragging it across the stage, I dodged the area left wet from the Gargling Olympics. Only minutes before, campers had gargled water while simultaneously humming jaunty tunes likc "The Star-Spangled Banner" and "Jingle Bells." Water dribbled down their fronts, drenching their T-shirts and tank tops. During the game, a desperate plea for laughter was quenched; minutes later, I could only hope a different kind of desperation would start to feel filled.

The giant box became the focal point of Night Three, my accompanying words an invitation to imagine what I described as the greatest gift humankind had ever been given. Unbeknown to many of the campers, I began to quote different bits and pieces of Scripture: God loved us so much (John 3:16) that he came and moved into the neighborhood (John 1:14). The Word—the history and the singular God the people had already *been* believing in—became flesh and dwelt among us (John 1:14 again). Because this same God, I probably said, sent his son, a real god-man named Jesus down to earth. And this God, this man, this *Jesus* was the image of the invisible God, the firstborn of all creation (Colossians 1:15). "He was fully God and fully man—100 percent God and 100 percent man," I regularly took to saying because "this Jesus was *God* in the *bod.*" By now, I was getting excited, worked up by mathematical theologies that didn't quite make sense in my brain while quoting tried-and-true expressions for the Son of God. Did I point to the enormous box as I said these words? Did I lean into its side, pushing into its sharp corners in order to make my point known?

Sometimes, now, I close my eyes and revisit the faces of those who sat before me, of the thousands of campers who heard these stories over the years. I think about how I worked my eyeballs across the crowd, perhaps imploring young ones into belief through intentional, prolonged eye contact—daring them to *just believe* by the power of a good story and of a storyteller who knew how to weave her way through the basics of delivering a message. Every single word mattered, each sentence a thread weaving into the next, emphatic point.

"Friends," I would say, "it's almost as if God was saying, 'Hey! Hey, you! Look! Look what I have for you. The greatest gift I could ever give you is right here. It's my son.'" I probably connected the dots from a story of long ago to today, from a gift given to the Israelites two thousand years ago and to us present-tense humans now. But I didn't stop there: I told them a story of Jesus as a grown-up and of a time he stumbled up on a short man who had climbed onto the low-hanging branches of a sycamore tree. Even though the man tried to play a little hide-and-go-seek with Jesus, he apparently wasn't very good at playing the game because Jesus found him right away.

"Zaccheaus!" Jesus hollered into a thick covering of light-green leaves. "Come down from that tree. Let's go to your house for dinner!" I would unpack the words and actions of Jesus, telling the students that Zacchaeus was the worst of the worst—a swindling, no-good, lying-stealing-cheating tax-collecting scoundrel of a human being. But this was the same man Jesus chose to eat dinner with that night—the same man the Biggest Gift of All called a *friend*.

Jesus showed the short man that he belonged, even if he'd gotten it wrong a time or two before. And Jesus, as it turned out, believed the same might be true for the rest of us too.

/ / /

I stare at the words written above, words uttered a thousand times before: I referred to God by male pronouns alone and threw sticky theological math equations into the slop bucket with the rest of the dining hall leftovers. When it came to semantics, I believed exclamation points, adverbs, and passive sentences an essential part of language and turned at least a head or two with that catchy phrase *God in the bod*. But are my beliefs about Jesus all that different nearly fifteen, twenty years later? Jesus. *Jesus*. His is the name I mutter when I stub my toe, when I am least aware: taken by surprise, the name *Jesus* is the first to pop out of my mouth, sometimes, now, accompanied by a rather uncouth string of expletives. His name is so automatic to my personhood, so ingrained within me, I don't know an existence *without* his name—for his is a name I've known ever since I knelt by the side of my bed in an attic bedroom on the Oregon coast.

"I wanna ask Jesus into my heart, Mama," my five-year-old self said one evening. My mother told me to do as she did, to say as she said. We got down on our knees and clasped our hands together in prayer. Closing our eyes, we whispered words to a man who somehow magically morphed his way into my heart. I remember jumping up from my kneeling spot on the side of the bed and running to grab my stick pony on the other side of the slanted-ceiling room. *Jesus lives in my heart! Giddy up, giddy up!* I shouted. Galloping around the room, I whooped and hollered, a holy bout of cowgirl's delight all mine until the stick pony bucked into a porcelain tea set. Pieces scattered across the room. Tears streamed down my cheeks. I didn't call out to Jesus, at least not in that moment, at least not yet.

Forty years later, the life of faith doesn't feel as easy as it used to be—the name of Jesus now layered within a journey of belief and disbelief, of running away from God and being pulled toward God in synchronous moments along the way. I suppose the Jesus of my church camp days is still there: his compassionate love the one my inner compass points toward, his fierce justice the guide I try to follow. But Jesus is no longer the tool I use to prove an equation correct or the name I use to draw divided boundary lines between who's in and who's out. No longer is he the one whose name I employ for positions of place within an inner circle or for decisions of who remains on the outside of understanding. This Jesus comes not with warnings or caveats of belonging, for he is no longer the one in whose name harm is done, for whom exclusion becomes the rule. I believe in a Jesus who does no harm.

/ / /

When I announced the idea of a book about church camp on social media, a follower on Instagram immediately messaged me in response: "*You should interview my friend Harmony*," she wrote. I reached out to Harmony, or, perhaps, Harmony first reached out to me. When we finally lined up a time to chat, I realized how right they were to suggest their name.

When Harmony Hookham-Dees (who uses *they/them* pronouns) was ten years old, they moved to a new city. Harmony's parents signed them up for church camp, not because the family was particularly religious, per se, but as a way to meet new people. I think about how often this rationale is used to *get* people into church settings: although the intention is good, it often turns out badly. A bait-and-switch kind of friendship might draw people in but is just as quickly snatched away when or if they end up leaving. Then the promise of belonging just as soon disappears. For Harmony, the ploy for connection worked, at least for a while. They remember arriving at camp for the first time: two "agents," camp counselors dressed in black suits and white shirts, stood at a set of closed gates. As each camper arrived, the agents would check to see if the child was on the list. I smiled, fingers furiously typing: I could imagine the scene perfectly, often curating scenes like this myself. But as a former military kid, Harmony didn't know what was happening in the moment: "Oh my God, what am I getting myself into right now? I'm out: I don't want any part of it!" When the agents ushered Harmony's car through the gates (and into a *Mission Impossible*-themed week of camp), Harmony quickly caught on. They couldn't get enough of the place or of the people.

During one of the obstacle course events later that night, Harmony's cabin stumbled across a typewriter with a hidden message on a strip of paper beside it. After their cabin decoded "top-secret information" by typing onto the paper, Harmony tore up and swallowed the sheet whole rather than throwing it away. The man in black stared at them. "Well, I had this trash can right here," he said, alluding to the paper they had just ripped into tiny pieces and swallowed. "That's not good enough," Harmony remembers saying. Both of us were laughing by this point in the story, their retelling of the memory a genuine boost to our spirits. As I wiped away tears, they explained how seriously they took camp, embracing the ethos of camp in an imaginary, creative sort of way. This trajectory continued for the next eight years as they returned to this same camp every summer and to a people who thought and believed like they did. Because at camp, Harmony knew they weren't alone, this formative place deep in the Shawnee National Forest their reset button for the year. As they said in one of our phone calls, "It didn't matter what had happened during the year because camp was how I realigned myself through the

Christian lens. Camp was how I viewed myself in Christ or God. I would drop everything that was stressing me out and leave it outside the campgrounds." Church camp became the place that directed Harmony's faith journey because it provided them with a place that accepted them for exactly who they were, or at least who they understood themselves to be at the time.

But when Harmony came out as bisexual after high school graduation, everything changed. Word spread quickly in their small town. The camp director—who had welcomed them to camp for nearly a decade as a camper and eventually as a junior counselor—banned them from camp property and from participating in any camp-affiliated events off property. The same man who stood outside a set of closed gates, begging them to accept their "mission, should they so choose," who continually preached a message of belonging and claimed that "it didn't matter your background, [for] God loves you and you have a place here," kicked Harmony to the curb. He shamed them for a decision that was never theirs to make in the first place. He shamed them in the name of Jesus.

Silence hung in the air, the weight of Harmony's story a boulder pushed down the side of a mountain. It filled a two-ton space between us. I knew my invitation was to hold their words, to listen and lean into the pain and let their sacred story change me—but sometimes I just want to hear the good parts of camp. I want cemented memories of belonging and of a God who loves and accepts every camper for exactly who they are, as they are. But these are not going to be the stories that change me or any of us, for that matter. When Harmony, who now identifies as a nonbinary, gender-fluid, bisexual person, looks back on their years at camp, they realize the effort they put into camp happened because they were overcompensating for something they felt was wrong with them. It took decades to unlearn shame and redefine their experiences at camp—to see themselves no longer as a belonger but as an outlier. For Harmony, their good experiences at camp "almost, not quite, now outweigh the negative impact." As they reflected on that time of their life, I could only nod my head in response. Church camp was such a *win* to me: I thrived in the camp environment, and camp, in turn, saw to my flourishing. But I was also exactly who white evangelicalism sought to promote: white and straight, I fit the mold. Outgoing and extroverted, I fought for my place as a woman, which camp rewarded me for when I proved I could *do* as the men had always done. But this was not the case for everyone.

"It's an honor to hold your words, Harmony," I finally said. "Thank you." They nodded their head. There wasn't a whole lot else to say during our time together.

I wish I could believe Harmony's experience an exception to the rule, but discrimination toward the LGBTQ+ community isn't anything new, particularly within the walls of the Church. Deborah Jian Lee, author of *Rescuing Jesus*, writes the following: "For outsiders to evangelical culture, it can seem absurd that a school can hire, fire, admit, and expel based on sexual orientation and not be in violation of nondiscrimination policies. But as *private, religious, educational* institutions, Christian schools are within their legal rights to pick and choose whom they let in and kick out. And in the wake of the Supreme Court's *Hobby Lobby* ruling, more institutions are demanding religious exemptions from laws and asserting that their discriminatory practices count as protected religious expression."[1]

Although Jian Lee speaks specifically about the private Christian school sector, the same applies to private and religious institutions such as church camps that often act under denominational or nonprofit religious status. Sexual orientation *can* very well be a factor in hiring decisions or exclusion clauses, which is why the ACA recommends individual camps take a close look at their "mission statement, its employee and camper handbooks, and any other written materials, including your position descriptions"[2] in order to avoid running afoul of anti-discrimination laws while also excluding certain people from being hired. Many white evangelical church camps discriminate against queer communities not only because they *can* (and their religious beliefs that homosexuality is wrong or sinful validate such discrimination) but also because "LGBTQ equality threatens their religious freedom," even if "what's at peril is not religious freedom but their ability to discriminate while receiving government support."[3]

What happens as a result? They do not allow a transgender boy to stay with his male peers in a boys' cabin,[4] or they terminate staff members on the spot if their sexual orientation does not align with policy standards.[5] They do not allow veteran senior staff to return, due to their sexuality,[6] or they assign young, effeminate male staff members they think "might be struggling with their sexuality" to hard labor because "it's what the child needs."[7] Like all religious organizations, they demand adherence to strict morality clauses from those who seek seasonal (and year-round) employment, clauses that often include beliefs, tenets, and policies around human sexuality. But many of these camps are fighting a losing battle. In truth, church camps are going to have "at least one youth or adult who identifies as lesbian, gay, bisexual, transgender, or queer"[8] every week during the summer. With LGBTQ+ youth coming out at earlier ages than previous generations and with growing societal acceptance toward the queer community, Deacon Ross Murray, camp director at The Naming Project, a Christian ministry serving youth of all sexual and gender identities, says there's only one thing church camps can do: acknowledge them and make efforts in creating safe spaces for them.[9]

On a whim, I emailed Ross to see if he might be interested in sharing more about the organization with me. When we met, he was warm and affable; his quick wit dared me finish my cup of coffee so as not to miss a single word.

"Camps are a set-apart place for the rest of the world," he mused. "Comparable to the mountaintop experiences, camps are weird and special. And they're designed to be that way." For many of the LGBTQ+ youth Ross works with at camp, removing themselves from family, school, and the pressures of normal, everyday life lets them explore new avenues and adventures. Maybe they try out a new name for the week. Maybe they let go of the ongoing pressure they constantly feel to *be* or act in a certain way around certain groups of people. Whatever their story, Ross and his team seek to provide inclusive boundaries and safety measures for the campers.

To Ross, their response is rooted in the heart of the ELCA (Evangelical Lutheran Church in America) tradition. For The Naming Project, which started with a grant to create inclusive camping options for BIPOC, the LGBTQ+ community, and those who are disabled, a heavy dependence on grace means believing humans can do or say nothing to earn anything from God. All is then a gift; everything *becomes* a gift. Instead of resisting change (including a change in increasing numbers of queer-identifying individuals), their team adopts and adapts their offerings; instead of doing nothing, they do something for a demographic that has often been forgotten in the church camp world.

"Evangelical camps want you to change for them more than they want to change for you," Ross finally stated when I circled back to an earlier point. His words stopped me in my tracks: how often did I expect others to change for me, for *my* offerings, and for my interpretations of a man named Jesus, more than I was willing to change for them?

Our short time together sticks with me long after we finished talking. It's obvious the organization is doing something right—something other camping ministries might dare steal and emulate, if they can. A prayer from one former camper solidifies this thought:

> *Stop the hate.*
> *Feed the hungry.*
> *Accept the differences.*
> *Open your arms to all.*
> *Bless the broken.*
> *Forgive the sorry.*[10]

Murray is not the only one who's trying to create safe havens for youth who do not identify as straight. In 2020, when Beyond Malibu, a wilderness adventure branch of Young Life, featured a promotional picture of a former guide and assistant director whose contract had not been renewed due to her sexual orientation, a close friend and former coworker named Kent Thomas started the Do Better Young Life (#DoBetterYoungLife) campaign and hashtag in response.

Many of Kent's earliest memories are associated with the organization, including weekly club meetings and monthly leadership gatherings that his parents hosted in their home, as well as camps he attended in various capacities through his early twenties. But when Kent came out at twenty-four, he messaged the national office to see if he could still be involved with the ministry. In an email exchange from 2015, Young Life responded with the following statement: "I'm sorry to hear that you're disappointed with Young Life after your decision [to come out as gay] last January. I would like to share more of why we have certain leadership expectations. Young Life's Faith and Conduct policy, which you likely saw as a Beyond guide, includes a Sexual Conduct Policy for those in leadership positions. This policy affirms the belief that we are created to experience sexual intimacy in the context of a marriage relationship between a man and a woman and those serving in leadership are expected to live within the context of this understanding."

The dismissive response didn't come as a surprise to him: he knew the organization's policies and knew he would not be welcomed as a full member of the community. But when his friend's picture was featured in the promotional material five years later, the image hit a nerve. He knew more stories needed to be heard, and ultimately, he saw it as an opportunity to provide a platform for queer people to be seen.

"'Do Better Young Life' came to mind because it's both an invitation and a demand," he explained when I interviewed him. "Young Life absolutely needs to change, and our stories are proof of that. I've been astonished by all the posts and private messages from people who have been harmed by Young Life's policies and actions, who have been hurt at places like camp, places that should be a place that does no harm." In less than a month, an Instagram account of the same name garnered nearly seven thousand followers, with hundreds of individuals "advocating for the intersectional inclusion of all people who have been harmed by Young Life."

Half a decade later, the organization has not changed its policy on human sexuality. But Kent continues to advocate for transparency and inclusion for current and future campers and staff members who don't yet know its harm.

/ / /

Now for the biggest irony of all: I introduced children and teenagers to a man I claimed as the greatest gift of all, a teacher and friend who loved more than anyone else. This version of Jesus was, at least in theory, centered in inclusion and embrace, "not simply to the religious and the privileged, but to the poor, the marginalized, the lonely and the left out."[11] Without exception or expectation, Jesus extended the wildest of welcomes and invitations to belonging—but in this particular church camp environment, belonging came with its own set of caveats. You belonged as long as you fit the mold, as long as you prayed the prayer, as long as you played by the rules.

I think about a statement I asked dozens of interviewees to answer: *True or false: church camp was made for white, straight, evangelical kids.* Unsurprising for a diverse group, their answers varied: Some waffled in their response, earnest for a third option that didn't throw those camps that *did* primarily serve white, straight, and evangelical campers under the bus. Others called me out on the pointedness of my statement: "Your position is clear when you ask us to make a choice here," one interviewee said. He believed I wouldn't voice such a strong opinion unless I believed it was true. "That could very well be the case," I replied. "So is the statement true? Is it false? Can you choose a side, even if you don't want to or don't agree with my position?" His lack of response became his answer. We moved on to the next question. Another man, a former high school camp director at a large nondenominational camp in Northern California, answered in the negative: during the summer months, the campers who came *were* largely white and evangelical, but during the year, a good number of conference center and weekend camp attendees didn't identify as white, let alone as evangelical. He seemed to think this modicum of diversity during the year was enough. I wasn't so convinced.

But for each of the queer-identifying individuals I interviewed, their response to the statement was a quick and emphatic "true!" "Church camp was created by white, straight evangelicals—that's its roots, stars, and origins," one respondent said. "Camp loses nothing if you decenter whiteness, straightness, and evangelicalism," someone else mused before wondering about how camps must have thought they'd lose *something* by such a decentering. Otherwise, why maintain power in the first place? Another interviewee, Sarah Powell, had been picking and choosing which questions to answer throughout our interview. But this particular question was one she felt she *had* to answer: "As a white, tried-to-be-straight kid for forty years of my life, I knew I couldn't be anything other than that at camp—and that's also why I couldn't be truly myself," Sarah said.

Church camp became a part of Sarah's life when she started attending FCA meetings and camps in middle school and high school. An athlete herself, she became a recreation major in college and spent five summers interning at a competitive Christian sports camp before dedicating the next twenty years of her life to camping ministries.

At the sports camp, Summer's Best Two Weeks, Sarah recalled how the camp motto, "I'm third," permeated the property: there, campers and staff practiced putting God first, others second, and yourself third on the field, in cabins, and even during meals. "One night, twelve of us were sitting around a big dinner table: two counselors and ten campers," Sarah explained. "There was this huge bowl of pudding with a little bit of whipped cream in the center of the table; naturally, someone asked if anyone wanted the whipped cream. When another person replied, 'I'm third,' that big bowl of pudding went around our table seven or eight times because we were all trying to be 'third' and not take too much." My jaw dropped to the ground: more than three decades have passed since Sarah worked at that camp, but the memory is clear as day for her—and it's one I can perfectly imagine happening in such a setting. "Everyone is trying to be so spiritual and Christlike, especially when this motto is fully integrated into the story of who Jesus is and who we're supposed to be as followers of him," she added. I could only nod my head by this point in our conversation. We sat in my backyard: twenty-six tomato plants surrounded us, bees buzzing and monarch butterflies flitting around worn and ratty deck chairs. The tiny urban farm I call home helped to draw out her stories—begging us stop and pause and reflect on nearly thirty years of friendship and on how two people can have two very different experiences of the same place.

Ten years my senior, Sarah was my boss my first two summers at camp. She taught me how to tie a bowline on a bight and how to rescue a camper on the high ropes course, should snaggletoothed danger ever occur. From her, I learned how to start a real campfire (build a pyramid) and how to squat and pee in the woods like a lady (on a large rock). When our friendship extended beyond summer camp and into "the real world"—wherein we worked in Christian environments, hung out with Christian friends, and lived with Christian roommates—we ate burritos from Taqueria Vallarta on Friday nights and camped at the Bowman Lake reservoir on long weekends. Her steady presence never waned, not when I moved away from California or when eventually she came out of the closet. Unlike Harmony, Sarah wasn't banned from camping ministries as much as she was pushed out of a position: church camp was a good fit until it wasn't. A number of camps had been her employers until a conflict with a new boss left her unemployed, questioning whether the environment was still right for her. It wasn't until she found a job outside the Christian bubble that she met gay people for the first time and eventually began to accept the truth about herself. For nearly four decades of her life, she had swallowed a narrative about the queer community, which is to say, about herself: They were bad and terrible people. They were wrong. They didn't belong. Statements made in the name of Jesus marked who she'd always been, even as she tried to fit into a mold of straightness. Aware of her attraction to women since she was a young girl, Sarah knew there wasn't room for this part of herself at church camp, at least not in an environment where heterosexuality is the only acceptable answer. So she pushed her sexuality to the back burner: as long as she belonged to this place, she refused to embrace her identity as a queer woman.

I think about this faithful friend whom my boys now call *auntie* and my husband refers to as *our people*. She belongs to us, and I think if asked the same question, she would say we belong to her. We hold an affinity toward one another because we make each other feel comfortable and at home—I accept her, and she accepts me, each as we are, expecting nothing in return. In this mutuality, we are linked together, even if the religious practices that brought us together in the first place no longer remain the glue that holds our sticky selves together. Theologian Erin S. Lane writes, "To 'get' to be ourselves means that belonging is both a gift we receive and a pilgrimage we make. To be our authentic selves requires some getting to, some working out, some traveling toward as we discern the 'me' we get to be. Learning to belong is lifetime work."[12] Funny how relationships at camp are often the opposite of lifetime work: Within days, you have twelve new best friends. Three weeks in, your heartbeats for the summer staffer you swear you'll someday marry. All the silliness and laughter of camp breaks down walls; the worship sessions and whisperings found under the stars are the same ones you won't be able to re-create two months later because that moment in time was gelled together by a powerful kind of Jesus-magic, impossible to create again. Church camp is a place like none other, and when you're in, you're in. But belonging almost functions like capital in the church camp world: it becomes transactional, a sort of demand and supply within the kingdom. In this world, you can have almost anything, if you pay the fee—and the fee, in this case, is having the right kind of belief. The fee is doing, saying, and speaking all the right things. If you do this, then you are rewarded. Then you belong. Then you can have it all, even if but for a brief window of time (and even if belonging comes with denying your personhood). I belonged in this place and to this place because I fit the mold. Unlike those in the queer community, I didn't have to give up a part of myself to leverage belonging to this place.

I stare at a cherry tomato plant in the distance behind Sarah Powell. A bee flits above her sandy-blond hair, buzzing around before swiveling back to a patch of tiny yellow flowers.

"Thank you, my friend," I say. "Not letting go of you yet." Wiping tears from our eyes, we walk back into the house.

/ / /

We return to the story of a short man, which is actually to say, of another, even greater man. When the Great Teacher peered through a thick covering of leaves, he saw Zaccheaus for who he actually was—a man he wanted to share a meal with, a man who was worthy of belonging. When you sit with this story for a minute or two, it's not hard to understand why Christians would believe Jesus the biggest and best present, the greatest gift of all. Now, make no mistake about the matter: I love me some Jesus. But Jesus isn't so much a shiny bauble to me anymore as much as he is a liberator and a blesser—a brown, colonized man "from a serially enslaved people, who lived in a time of occupation and colonization,"[13] who made it his business to bless "all the people this world has crushed," who found a way to center the people this world has marginalized, celebrate the people this world forgets, and validate the people this world invalidates.[14] Marked by a wild kind of inclusion, I pay attention to those on-the-ground stories of his humanness, when the fleshy stuff of God comes face to face with people of the ancient world.

The difference is not so much in the presentation of inclusion as much as it is in the manifestation *of* inclusion. Too often, the Jesus message of white evangelical church camp comes with its own set of rules. From the stage and from the front of the campfire pit, preachers tout a version of St. Luke's words to the church in Acts: "Believe in the Lord Jesus Christ and you will be saved"[15]—but the verse becomes a mangled version of assimilation. Believe in the Lord Jesus Christ, and you will give up your queerness. Believe in the Lord Jesus Christ, and you will follow (and, dare I say, want to become) a whitewashed version of Jesus. Believe in the Lord Jesus Christ, and you will give up your womanhood, demonstrating instead a "male-like leadership style—straight-shooting, confident, always on,"[16] for this is the type of leadership most valued in the Church. Void of culture and ignorant of diversity, this version of Jesus becomes more resemblant of a tan-skinned, pectoral-clad David Hasselhoff-type lifeguard running in the sand to save the whole of humanity from the possibility of drowning than the brown-skinned Jewish refugee, whose very experiences across borders allowed him to see the presence of God in all people. Simply put, the caveats attached to this Jesus mean assimilation into the values most cherished by white evangelicalism—that is to say, of a people most valued by the white evangelical church. If you do not identify as white, straight, or male, then this Jesus does not sit at the foot of your sycamore tree, nor will he ever be inviting you to dine at his house.

Who, then, is the Jesus we can invite campers to know on the third night of camp? I'd like to think it's the same one who greets you at the door after a long time away. Even if you haven't seen him in a while, you know him; even if this is the first time ever bumping into him, there is a knowing, deep down inside—because he in turn knows you. He calls out your name; he embraces you in a squishy hug; he lets out a hearty guffaw at a long-forgotten memory you share. "Oh, it's *you*," he finally says, or perhaps you say it first. Together, you fit, and you know, for you simply *are* together. Because this unbounded Jesus comes from an unbounded kind of Christianity that's not about who's in and who's out but is instead about a particular direction in which you move. This Christ is less concerned with the boundaries of who we think we're supposed to be on the other side (or of who certain figureheads in the Church say we're supposed to be in order to fit in and belong) and more concerned with the whole of humanity.

Here, white evangelical camping ministries let go of bounded-set thinking and instead embrace centered-set thinking. One pair of theologians describe it as such:

> In some farming communities, the farmers might build fences around their properties to keep their livestock in and the livestock of neighboring farms out. This is a bounded set. But in rural communities where farms or ranches cover an enormous geographic area, fencing the property is out of the question. . . . Under these conditions a farmer has to sink a bore and create a well, a precious water supply. . . . It is assumed that livestock, thought they will stray, will never roam too far from the well, lest they die. This is a centered set. As long as there is a supply of clean water, the livestock will remain close by.[17]

When Christ is the well, "everyone is in and no one is out."[18] Artificial boundaries sometimes disguised as caveats of belonging are thrown out the window (or, for purposes of camp-speak, off the second platform on the high ropes course—you know, the one right before that unwieldy set of unstable bridges). This time, when a camp speaker introduces campers to a man who was the biggest gift of all, to the Tender Pioneer whose generous, wild inclusion paved a way for the rest of us to be equally generous and wild in the love we show other people, they actually mean it.[19] This time, the Harmonys and the Sarahs of this world are in; those who have been pushed to the sides and not let in the entrance gates of camp because of their genders and sexualities, their orientations and their queer identities, find belonging in the holy places where God and nature kiss. They belong simply because of the humans they are, simply because Love demands that everyone belongs.[20]

For this time, as we sing songs that sound best under a canopy of stars and listen to tales of a man who moved into the neighborhood[21] and became a real, live, fleshy example of love, joy, peace, patience, kindness, goodness, gentleness, and self-control,[22] we, too, discover our place in the story. We chuckle when we think about that big, fat red box of a gift we once dragged across the stage at camp, not because the illustration is extreme but because we'd still drag an old refrigerator box plastered in Costco-sized wrapping paper across the stage today, if given the chance. For on each of the campers in that place, Christ places a cap of belonging: on those campers with loads of faith, who know the words to every song and practice hand motions during the school year, and on those who would like to have more; on those who are coming to camp for the very first time, who haven't yet made a "camp best friend," and on those who sport T-shirts from the past seven years; on those who haven't stepped through the gates of camp for a very long time (but still yearn to be accosted by a "Secret Service agent"); on every camper, past, present, and future, who has tried to follow Jesus, and on those campers who have failed every single time.[23] To each one of these campers, we attach belonging as, together, we move in the direction of the one who is the center.

4

Dirty Rotten Little Sinners

On the fourth night of camp, I would often tell one of my favorite stories and crack open a can of slimy, theological worms as a result. As the story goes, when I was a freshman in high school, my friend and I had the brilliant idea to hop a fifteen-foot-tall chain-link fence at the back of our school's football field. She turned out to be a professional fence-hopper, or so it seemed, ascending and descending the fence in approximately 3.4 seconds. I turned out to be more of a fence-trier: seven minutes in, when I finally reached the top of the fence and proceeded to lop one leg over the horizontal metal pole, my long, D. J. Tanner-like sweater and matching white stretch pants turned against me. The spiky metal twists at the top of the fifteen-foot fence refused to release their grip. The spikes did not let up, not when my fake penny loafers tried to kick their way out nor when my Esprit bag, loaded with a barrage of textbooks, flapped in the breeze, heavy fabric thumping against metal—nor even when all three of the high school football teams stopped their afternoon practices to watch the girl who was stuck at the top of a fence.

"I was stuck, helpless," I would say to the campers. "There was nothing I could do to get over the fence. I was *helpless* on my own." I didn't have to tell them, at least not yet anyway, that my friend quickly ascended and descended the fence a second time, while I made my way back down the way I came up. A couple hundred yards later, we found a hole in the fence—a hole big enough for both of us to walk through, unencumbered by Esprit bags, ruined stretch pants, and bloody hands. I didn't always tell campers this part of the story because it wasn't the point or the end goal; the point was that I was stuck and helpless. "The Bible calls that stuck situation *sin*," I would declare. "We try and fix this problem of feeling stuck on our own. We feel hurt, but really we're living life on our own, apart from God. We're separated from God—that's the definition of sin. Each one of us has sinned, and each one of us has gone our own way. *Each one of us is stuck* in this thing called *sin*."[1]

I would often add that sin is real. Sometimes I would hold up a sign with the three-letter word *sIn*, with a little *s* and a little *n* overshadowed by a huge capital *I* in the middle: because when we sin, the *I* in *sin* is bigger and more important than anything else. "It's like saying what I want for my life is more important than what you want, God," I would often add.

An analogy, or two, also often accompanied this night: Sometimes I dragged two chairs across the stage. At first, the chairs faced one another as if to mimic a sit-down, face-to-face conversation with another person. Although that's how chairs should functionally operate, something else happened when sin came into the picture. Sin turned the chairs around. Instead of the chairs facing one another as intended, the backs of the chairs faced one another. "It's like playing musical chairs without any of the benefits," I might add. "No loud music, no chair-wrestling to see who gets the seat, no coveted prize at the end." And then there were the years of dragging giant refrigerator boxes wrapped in red wrapping paper across the stage. Here, a demonstration for sin wasn't too hard: I could just push or throw the gift to the back of the stage. (Letting the results of "sin" tip off the *front* of the stage, into the laps of unsuspecting campers or into a blazing campfire pit, would have made for excellent dramatics but was, admittedly, a little *too* over the top.)

Whatever the analogy, the sin talk had to end at some point. Far from feeling like a beloved child of God, campers instead left feeling the weight of the human condition—which was, of course, the entire point. Because within this framework, every person in that place *had* to feel the heftiness and consequences of sin in order for God to whip out a Savior-Son and solve the problem a night later. I would often end the night by equating sin to a virus that runs inside each one of us, deep inside our bodies. "We're all infected with this virus, with this separation from God, even if the symptoms come out differently," I would somberly declare. No sooner than I began ticking off symptoms of the virus—lying to your parents, smoking pot, sleeping around, getting drunk as a skunk—I'd put one last nail in the coffin and end the night with a reminder that "the wages of sin is death."[2] The consequence of this virus was death, plain and simple. It's almost as if I *wanted* these children and youth to leave feeling like worthless pieces of trash, left to rot and mold and disintegrate in the balmy heat. *Left to your own devices, child, you're going to destroy yourself. And there's nothing you can do about it.*

/ / /

Just as we spent three nights welcoming campers in, inviting them to see God, begging them to take another look at a man named Jesus, we took a U-turn on Night Four. *Beloved*, I'd called them because they were. *Child of God*, I'd said because they needed to hear it. Now I'd gone and smacked them upside the head by reminding them of their dirtiness, their sinfulness, and the inevitable sad piece of the human puzzle they could do nothing to solve. Ignoring the words and actions of Jesus, I'd taken to channeling a couple of sentences from St. Paul the apostle before sadly telling them about the burning, sulfurous place they'd someday come to call home. How dramatic it would have been to shake my fists in the air and shout, "Damn the curse of humanity!" but since we weren't supposed to curse at church camp, it was like I started calling them by a new name instead: *dirty rotten little sinner*. Even if I didn't actually say this into the microphone (and instead simply called them *sinner*), this new name faithfully communicated the truth of our human selves.

Lest you think I am exaggerating, consider how Protestant founding father Martin Luther called himself "a filthy, stinking bag of worms"[3] or how sixteenth-century revivalist Jonathan Edwards dazzled audiences with sentences like "The God that holds you over the pit of hell, much as one holds a spider; or some loathsome insect, over the fire, abhors you and is dreadfully provoked."[4] Because the concept of human depravity—"the Calvinist doctrine that human nature is thoroughly corrupt and sinful as a result of the Fall"[5]—is baked into the framework of white evangelicalism, this particular interpretation of sin is essential for the sequence to be successful. We desperately *want* to get to the correct answer: we want to get to Jesus. But we cannot get to him if we don't play by the rules—which in this case means accepting that if you "sin, refuse to repent, harden your heart, reject Jesus, [then] when you die, it's over. Or actually, the torture and anguish and eternal torment will have just begun."[6] Add in a number of questionable illustrations used to explain sin (solely on a personal, individualistic level, I might add), and the party is just getting started.

Many of the former campers I interviewed recalled speakers using the two chairs, while others recalled pieces of paper being ripped in half. One woman wrote, "I remember being told that I am a sinner, and sin smells and God doesn't want to be around sin. Camp staff would tell us, 'You get up in God's nose,' and hold a snotty, crumpled-up tissue toward the audience." A number of folks recall plastic pitcher analogies in which pitchers became symbols of purity and pollution, of righteousness and sin. A speaker would hold up a pitcher, often filled halfway with water. Into it, they would pour food coloring, juice, a box of cereal, a cup of slop from the food waste bucket, a scoop of dirt from the ground—really, anything they could get their hands on to make the contents inedible and dirty. *Would you want to drink from this pitcher?* they would ask campers, slowly showcasing the goopy liquid from one side of the stage to the other. *Neither does God.* (The same gross pitcher would often return a night later, only to be replaced by a pitcher of clear, unsullied water. In this example, Jesus becomes the Great Purifier. Through him, the analogy goes, God makes the dirty water clean again.) Halfway through the week, sin became a trump card to evangelical belief systems, a scare tactic often used to frighten kids into making the only right choice.

The problem, of course, is that sin wasn't the most important thing to Jesus. He really wasn't interested in defining people by their sinfulness but by their belovedness. Nevertheless, white evangelical church camps tend to focus on concepts of human depravity when it comes to explaining *how* Jesus did what he did on the cross. Called *penal substitution* for short, or the *penal substitutionary atonement* if you really want to put your dancing shoes on, according to one writer from The Gospel Coalition, this theory "holds that the most fundamental event of the atonement is that Jesus Christ took the full punishment that we deserved for our sins as a substitute in our place, and that all other benefits or results of the atonement find their anchor in this truth."[7] Put another way, in this belief system, the only way to make Jesus the missing puzzle piece to the problem of sin a night later is to first understand the phrase "full punishment that we deserved for our sins."[8] It's to turn a message of a loving God who says, "*You are beautiful and you are loved*" into a transaction. According to this view, because "Jesus paid the penalty for sin in a legal sense, purchasing our redemption at the cost of his blood,"[9] humans are left with no other choice. They have to make right a wrong. But until this right-making happens, campers get to feel like a piece of shit, even if just for a night.

/ / /

At what point does staking claim to an atonement theory, such as penal substitutionary atonement, cross the line? When do good intentions instead result in further harm, let alone psychological and spiritual damage? For me, when early research efforts didn't yield answers as to the damage absorbing such a theory actually *does* to children and youth, specifically in church camp settings, I thought it best to approach the situation with a little bit of humor. I did what I tend to do when the setting gets tough: I tried to add levity to an otherwise dire situation, one last Hail Mary of an attempt to find laughter in between the cracks of a poor, fear-based theology. And so I imagined a little story, rooted in journalism and best suited for publication at a completely legitimate news source like *The Onion*:

> Penal substitutionary atonement, an atonement theory widely embraced by a number of conservatives, mostly within the Reformed tradition, is damaging children and youth at record numbers. A robust presence within much of white evangelicalism, its tenants are regularly preached from the pulpit, taught in Sunday school classes, and stated in bold font on the "What We Believe" section of church websites.
>
> The atonement theory capitalizes on making people feel like a piece of shit in order to understand their need for God. Nowhere is this felt more than during the summer months, when thousands of children and youth attend church camps across the US.
>
> "If I can make children feel dirty and worthless, then I've done my job," Larry Goberry, a veteran camp speaker said. "They only have to marinate in their dirtiness for a day, sometimes even half a day, but then they're primed and ready to hear the Good News!" According to Goberry, even though their worthlessness prevents them from having a relationship with God, children and youth don't need to worry about anything.

"God loves you so much he killed his only son!" Goberry added. "That's the Good News!"

The harmful theology is particularly damaging to those under the age of eighteen. Not only do they grow up believing God's love is conditional and remain prone to guilt-induced, works-based models of faith, but they believe themselves worthless sacks of garbage.

"I'm a dirty rotten little sinner!" A ten-year-old girl shouted, as she stepped off the bus from summer camp.

"I'm a worthless piece of shit!" A seventeen-year-old boy added, high-fiving her at the bottom of the steps.

Opponents urge the Church to stop flipping the switch on God's love and put an end to penal substitutionary atonement as a way of explaining the cross. Although the theory tends to work in the short-term, the outdated model ends up doing more harm than good. Record numbers of former campers are leaving the faith, report low self-esteem, and continue to unpack the harmful theology long into adulthood.

Proponents remain unconvinced.

"Why change what works?" One pastor stated in response to the accusation.

Church camps refused to comment, when asked.

I hoped the imagined scene would give readers enough of a base as to the harmful effects that often exist for young people when they're forced to toggle between dueling realities. On the one hand (or in the case of camp, on the one *day*), campers receive a message of unending, abounding love: *God loves you more than anything else.* Then the script is flipped: *But God believes you are dirty and worthless, a sinner in every sense of the word.* A day (or in some cases, a half a day later), a solution to the contradictive *but* emerges through a "God who can only effect the salvation of sinners through an act of violent retribution."[10] But the effects are nonetheless jarring, both in the immediate and in the aftermath, often years and decades later. Harsh chords of cognitive dissonance begin to play their haunting tune when campers are forced to wrestle with these realities, both of what this great and perfect deity supposedly believes about them and also of what this means they should believe about themselves.

Lest the reader think I have wandered too far off course, consider the following answers to one of the questions I asked interviewees: *What was the theology communicated or that you perceived at camp?*

- "Jesus saved you from an angry God. You were saved from going to hell."—James
- "You're dirty, but don't worry, God loves you so much that he killed his only son."—Holly
- "Jesus loves me but his dad thinks I'm a piece of shit."—Kent
- "I'm a wretched sinner and I don't exist. And I cannot exist without God."—Jessica

- "You're bad. God has to have atonement for your sin. So, God's going to send his son, but because God is good, everything's going to turn out all right if you just say yes."—Billy Jack
- "You're a sinner and you're dirty and God's love can't get to you anymore."—Sarah

It's no wonder a get-saved mentality often exists in such an environment: when humans feel robbed of the very goodness that lives within them, that *is* inherently them, of *course* they're going to want to do anything in their power to make right the wrong—including any wrongs they've come to believe about themselves, deep down inside. Of *course,* they're going to want to return to a place that centers itself on an orbiting, all-consuming kind of love instead of on pounding threats of hate, shame, and guilt from a wrathful God dead set on getting his way. Because when the dissonance between the reality of a loving God who also thinks you're a piece of trash becomes part of the framework of white evangelicalism, "you put human beings in two categories: the saved and the damned, the beloved and the hated."[11] Is it any wonder that former campers and camp staff members feel harmed by the theology they preached, damaged by the singular message they received?

For Jo Luehmann, writer and host of The Living Room podcast, penal substitutionary atonement is nothing short of abusive theology. The theory "teaches us that we are disgusting and gross and nothing but filthy rags—that God cannot look at us unless through the lens of Jesus," she posits in a Facebook video. "From the moment we were born, all that we are is just sinners. We are divorced from the beauty and the divinity that we were created in." As Luehmann further explains, this position doesn't merely affect how a camper sees God and themselves; it also affects how they see other people. It amplifies definitions of "the other," furthering "us and them" conversations that too often exist within religious circles. In this scenario, "those who don't share [our] same theological framework . . . become objects we have to save, people that we have to convince that they are gross and disgusting and need Jesus too badly."[12]

But for the psychologists and therapists among us, hearing such messages about God, self, and others can be a form of complex spiritual trauma. Just as complex trauma is repeated and prolonged (which is the case for campers who hear this message, year after year, or for those who go home to churches that regurgitate such beliefs), religious trauma is the "physical, emotional, or psychological response to religious beliefs, practices, or structures that overwhelm an individual's ability to cope and return to a sense of safety."[13] As Dr. Laura Anderson, a psychotherapist who specializes in helping clients heal from religious trauma, points out, the body's response *to* an "event, belief, practice, relationship, or structure may be so overwhelming that it circumvents our ability to naturally cope with what is going on and would not allow us to come back to a space of safety."[14] Campers, whether in the moment or years later, might experience pervasive feelings of helplessness, powerlessness, and shame; they might not be able to shake subsequent feelings of terror and fear, at least not when it comes to the messages they swallowed about their bodies or their relationships, their sexualities or their genders. Although religious trauma is often more subjective than it is objective, Anderson sums up this loss of safety with the following observation:

> Religious trauma can result from anything that is too much, too soon, or too fast in the context of religion that overwhelms your ability to cope and return to a sense of safety. This could be prompted by a single incident (think of a scary altar call!) or messages and experiences over the years (think of purity culture, messages of total depravity, or the doctrine of hell) that overwhelm us to the point where we are unable to cope or feel safe. The overwhelm could be prompted by something that others were not as impacted by or something that many were impacted by.[15]

I may have a tendency to try to laugh away the hard things in life, but I don't doubt the impact of hearing how you're just another dirty rotten little sinner, sometimes over and over again, very well may have resulted in eventual feelings of guilt and shame and unworthiness for some of the campers who swallowed the message hook, line, and sinker. In fact, I'd even go so far as to say we're hard-pressed not to admit the possibility exists in the first place.

/ / /

Of course, the fourth night of camp wasn't just about sin; it was also about the place all that sin supposedly sent you if you didn't say yes to Jesus by the end of the week. It was about hell.

"Hell was a real good whip-a-towel," one interviewee recalled. "A great way to scare the living shit out of you. I mean, surely, you'd pick and want to be a part of the opposite. It was the only alternative that makes sense." I think of the idiom of a carrot and a stick: if heaven is the carrot dangled before one donkey's nose to entice it forward, hell is the stick that thumps another donkey's rear end toward movement. As the original idiom suggests, the driver who beat his donkey with "blackthorn twigs" in order to win the race is the one who ends up losing, while the driver who enticed his jack forward with a root vegetable (sometimes a carrot, at other times a turnip) is declared the winner.[16] One used a method of reward and inspiration, the other a method of punishment and threat—both to induce a particular behavior or desired effect in their braying ass. Is it all that different when a majority of white evangelical church camps continue to employ similar idioms to move vulnerable children and adolescents toward conversion? Hell becomes a scare tactic used to instill fear—the stick that beats against a camper's young and formidable psyche. (The concept of heaven, on the other hand, which we will discuss in later chapters, becomes the dangling carrot, the future desired reward.)

Why continue to paint such monochrome pictures of faith and of the Christian life in general? Simply put, because it works. Fear is one hell of a motivator, for both the sender and the receiver. Within the framework of white evangelicalism, if you believe that God only opens wide the pearly gates to those who ABC (admit, believe, commit) their lives to Jesus, then you're going to do everything you can to make sure people at least *hear* about the golden ticket available to them. You want to be with all your peeps forever! You don't want to see them burn to death in a fiery inferno! As one theologian notes, "The sad thing is that some of my acquaintances, including many who lead entire churches, admit that if there was no hell, they would not follow Jesus and they would not bother telling others about him."[17] I doubt it's all that different for the millions of campers who attend white evangelical church camps each summer: when black-and-white dichotomies between heaven and hell are created, and heaven is not only depicted as the *only* answer that makes sense but also as the least scary option available, a camper is going to opt out of nightmares and eternal punishment. They're going to run far away from hell's beating stick. As it goes, threatening kids with hell is a conversion tactic that tends to get the job done, in seven days or less—and if church camps are in the business of bumping up the number of souls in heaven (which they are, with many camps requiring staff to count conversions at the end of each week so they can report those numbers to donors), then threatening hell is an easy way to tick those numbers up.

But, hell. How have we delved so deeply into grandiose ideas of the subject without having tried to understand whether it's a spiritually helpful (let alone theologically sound) option in the first place? I suppose the answer to that question entirely depends on whether or not you think heaven and hell are real, actual places real, actual humans go to after they die. Although there are fourteen references to hell in the New Testament, eleven of those references are said to have come from the mouth of Jesus himself and talk about a place human beings might just end up because of God's hateful judgment. Every time Jesus talked about this place called *hell*, he was talking about a desolate valley outside of town called Gehenna—and all of these references to Gehenna are completely apocalyptic in nature. They are "actually about the coming judgment on Israel, Jerusalem, and its temple."[18] Certainly, this would have been a huge deal to those who sat at the feet of Jesus and listened to what he had to say. But apocalyptic language is to literal language as apples are to oranges, as my fourth-grade soccer skills are to world-class athletes such as Kylian Mbappé.

When various theologians tried to make sense of the whole thing over the next two thousand years, different theories developed. Should one ascribe to infernalism, annihilationism, or universalism?[19] Of the first, is the tormented conscious at the time of torture, and is said tormenting a one-time deal or an everlasting, always-and-forever type of thing? As for the all-consuming fire: Is it in a lake, under the earth, or just made up of burning, sulfurous flames in general? Metaphorical interpretations notwithstanding, as far as timelines go, the Western Church and its Evangelical wing held on to viewpoints of infernalism since the fourth century, thanks to the influence of St. Augustine, the great Doctor of the Latin Church. Often touted as the most influential voice in Christianity since the apostle Paul, Augustine argued on the side of punitive judgment, spewing predictions of a day when "true and full happiness shall be the lot of none but the good, while deserved and supreme misery shall be the portion of the wicked, and of them only."[20] Soon enough, his views of an endless, sulfuric hell became the only biblical view of judgment and hell, used to further enflame "the early universalist Fathers as heretical and their modern proponents as liberal."[21] After his version of hell really took off, other writers threw their hats in the ring: Dante tried his hand at a rather fiery *Inferno* in 1314, and Milton soon followed suit with *Paradise Lost* nearly 350 years later. Not to be outdone, Jonathan Edwards built himself an empire on the backs of the wrathful place (and of an extremely wrathful, angry God) in 1741: "His wrath towards you burns like fire; he looks upon you as worthy of nothing else, but to be cast into the fire; he is of purer eyes than to bear to have you in his sight; you are ten thousand times more abominable in his eyes than the most hateful venomous serpent is in yours. You have offended him infinitely more than ever a stubborn rebel did his prince; and yet, it is nothing but his hand that holds you from falling into the fire every moment."[22] Bonus points for any readers who hold a pitchfork in one hand, a lighter in the other, and reread the above paragraph in your deepest, boomiest scary voice.

Perhaps it comes as no surprise that church camps took up the reins with a wide swath of questionable hell skits 250 years after the fact. While the music of Michael W. Smith and Jennifer Knapp played in the background, the hearts of campers started to churn—thanks, in part, to the threat of getting a one-way ticket to such a place in a handbasket. Newsboys, Audio Adrenaline, and Mercy Me soon followed suit, at least when it came to the musical aesthetics that helped create an ambiance of holy doom and fear. And many camps across theological spectrums even went so far as to ensure "messy games" happened on the same day as the sin talk, the theory being that if campers could experience the fullness of having oatmeal, mud, and shaving cream thrown at them, they could also understand the fullness of the mess sin had made in their lives. "It's messy because we get down deep into the lives of students' lives," one youth pastor said of the good, clean messy games they played at church camp.[23] Whatever the dramatic interpretation, two things were sure: its theology would no doubt be faulty, but it sure would do the trick. Campers would be scared into saying a big, fat "hell, no!" every single time.

/ / /

A man named Jeff McSwain wanted to do something about the problem of harmful messaging. But flipping the script on constructs of sin and hell isn't always accepted within the walls of white evangelicalism. Instead, it can sometimes mean getting fired the fast way. It can mean losing everything you've always known.

In truth, I had known Jeff's name long before I actually engaged with the gentle, soft-spoken man. In 2007, I was on staff with Young Life, an international youth outreach organization, when his name made headlines. According to Jeff, it was a controversy over theological belonging: If all people belonged to God, they shouldn't have to *believe* in order to belong in the first place. Instead, they belonged to God *so that* they might someday believe. In the end, Young Life unflinchingly held to its own scriptural perspective and to evangelical roots that declared one must first believe in order to belong to God as a child.

Two years into my time with the organization, I was still somewhat of a newbie. Even though I had been involved with the institution since high school, Young Life still felt like a shiny bauble to me—the ultimate of youth ministries. I believed it a place that did camping like nobody's business, a ministry whose model of introducing adolescents to the person of Jesus Christ could do no wrong. When it came to theology, Young Life had a tried-and-true *way* of presenting the gospel that just worked—a way of presenting the gospel that is now mimicked in the chapters of this book, even if parts of its presentation are universal across much of white evangelical camping. As staff members, we employed this strategy across a semester's worth of weekly "club" meetings, we condensed it into a four-part series at fall and winter weekend camps, and we expanded it to seven messages during a week of summer camp. For a long time, there was room for a speaker to experiment and try new things, to dip their toes into the waters of Barth or to walk through the Old Testament in order to see Jesus anew.

By the time *Jeff McSwain* became a household name, Young Life had already begun to insist on a turn-or-burn proclamation theology[24]—which is to say that proclaiming the gospel for the worldwide organization began to mean starting people off in hell, separated from God because of their sin. This lawbreaking on behalf of humanity required punishment: only *if* Jesus died, and then only *if* people repent and believe, do they get saved. Jeff simply solidified the deal by daring to preach a message of belonging before belief. "Are we to tell them they belong to Jesus *if*. . .?" Jeff asks in an article for *Other Journal*. "Is belonging with an *if* really belonging at all?"[25] To Jeff, this was unconditional belonging without being a universalist. Universalism doesn't need Jesus, for all are simply saved. But Jeff's theology still reeked of a singular pointedness to Jesus and a wildly inclusive, albeit narrow, path to God. By daring to preach a message of belonging before belief, Jeff provoked Young Life to double down on the necessity of penal substitutionary atonement.

It didn't go well.

Of course, Jeff's firing—and Young Life's subsequent top-down proclamation of a singular way of presenting the gospel—didn't happen overnight. Early in 2000, during a seminary course, no less, he had an epiphany that changed his life forever: While walking on the beach in Daytona Beach, Florida, he began to see every person on that beach as a child of God. Man, woman, child, it didn't matter who they were. It didn't matter whether they believed or didn't believe in a message of the Christian God—Jeff believed every person was a child of God, not because of any truths created out of belief but simply because of the truth of Jesus. In more ways than one, this flipped Jeff's theology around. Instead of starting with Protestant understandings of human depravity and separation from God, Jeff began echoing the early church fathers who made universal claims about Jesus as the Second Adam, in whom all humans were included—who had already called him, and every stranger walking on that beach, a *beloved child*.

By the time Jeff spoke at Frontier Ranch, which he describes as the Rose Bowl of all Young Life camps, that summer, he had switched everything around. He spelled it out for me when we spoke over Zoom: "Instead of sin separating us from God, we belong to Jesus because of what *he* has already done. Sin is not then about breaking God's law, but it's about fighting against the embrace of the One who loves us most." In a nutshell, Jeff didn't play by the rules. He didn't employ Young Life's suggested model of how (and when) a speaker should present a message of God's unconditional love. By giving up the psychological pressure to start campers off in a state of hell, separated from God, he did not get as many teenagers to stand up at "Say So" at the end of the week—a night when campers have the opportunity to stand up and "let the redeemed of the Lord say so,"[26] by making a public declaration of their faith. This was worrisome to those who expected a higher number of converts, who were used to teenagers responding in a certain way to a certain order of talks.

He scratched the stubble on his face as he mused over the apparent trouble he caused nearly twenty years ago: "If you don't start people off in hell, the ones who hear the message don't get quite as worried. Starting campers off in the embrace of Christ, and as already belonging to God as children, is not your typical fear-based approach. But the truth is that people who come to Christ out of fear learn to hate their conversion. On the other hand, people who come to Christ out of love, love their conversion. They're the ones who stick with their faith, ten, twenty, thirty years later." As the story goes, Jeff was eventually put on probation: There was a right and a wrong way of doing things, and he had clearly landed in the wrong. Still, he dug in. He continued to employ a model critiqued as too universalist, too progressive, and too soft on sin, even as he spoke on a national level for several more years.

A glint appeared in Jeff's eyes as he recalled this story—but I couldn't tell if this twinkle was one of rebellion or warmth, smugness or pain. Perhaps a little bit of everything. Jeff would face criticism over the years, former fans, ministry associates, and friends echoing sentiments of what he *should* have done, of what he *could* have said.

"You know, we had a chance for these kids to be saved," he remembers one disgruntled staff member saying to him after he preached at camp during the summer. "But you didn't talk about sin in a way that really shook them up and made them realize they had a critical need."

By the time Young Life fired him in 2007, the national organization was clearly no longer behind him.[27] This is when our story originally intersected—not when I sat with him face to face over a computer screen nearly twenty years later, hopeful at the power of our collective, intersecting stories and of a God who still looked on each of us and smiled, but when I sat in a large meeting room with dozens of other Young Life staff members in 2008. Each one of us was slated to follow in Jeff's footsteps and speak at camps across the country that summer. We were the cream of the crop, or so they told us. The chosen ones, the ones whose feet were most blessed because, of all the staff people around the world, we'd been picked as camp speakers. But Young Life wasn't going to pass us the microphone unless we promised to adhere to their messaging guidelines, unless we joined in the jeering crowd of those who threw Jeff McSwain's name under the bus because he dared to believe belonging might actually come before belief.

/ / /

I want to return to the scene of a girl stuck on the top of the fence. This time, I want to apply all those feelings of "stuckness," not to how we view sin but to how a summer staff crew might proceed when a director decides to buck tradition. I was twenty years old, working as a high ropes instructor for a second full summer at camp. Instead of letting the camp staff run with old song favorites, our director hired a former Disney songwriter and choreographer to teach all of us a new song called "The Alpha and Omega."[28] She thought singing about starships zooming through the sky, toward the Alpha and Omega, was a good idea; she didn't think the phrase "probe the final bend" might sound deliciously phallic to twentysomething-year-old college boys. Not only did this poor woman think the song and its terrible, accompanying motions would take us to the next level of performance and expertise, but she also didn't think the staff would revolt in return.

How wrong she was. I joined in the chorus of returning staff members: surely, it would be the beginning of our ruin, the destruction of everything good and holy and precious about the traditions of our precious little church camp. The drama lasted approximately five whole days, but such a number is equal to at least half a decade in the real world. In the end, we won the fight and didn't have to sing the song in any opening-day ceremonies that summer. But seeing as I can still sing every word of that blasted, planetary Jesus song nearly twenty-five years later, one has to wonder if the camp director actually won the war.

My point is this: more often than not, we know, deep down in our bones, that another, better way is possible. For those of us who still spend our summers at white evangelical church camps and continue to allow a message of dirty worthlessness to permeate the spaces we care deeply about, it's time to fight back. Even if we remain the lone staff member in an organization who refuses to ascribe to the same hate and exclusion the organization tacitly employs but continues to let harmful and archaic atonement models be the accepted way of communication, it's time to sing a new song. No more does the suggestion to seek another way apply to conversations of sin and hell, particularly in that sacred, outdoor space where heaven and earth collide.

I can't tell you what to teach, but I can tell you that in the last two chapters of Revelation, God hits the "restart button on the cosmos. Old is gone . . . new has come. The redemption of all things visible and invisible, earthly and heavenly has come" to a beautiful and final end because of Jesus.[29] All that stuff that came before—including old interpretations and worn-out models of getting people to believe what you want them to believe and do things in a certain way because that's just the way it's done—no longer matters anymore.

Instead, what matters in this scenario is that Jesus is the radiance. And this radiance changes everything. It's like using your favorite filter on a photograph: suddenly, the blemishes blend into the background, and the wrinkles smooth away, and the tired bagginess under your eyes just isn't a thing anymore. The filter changes everything, even if just for a moment in time. But the filter doesn't erase the reality of the picture: Sin is still there—in fact, you might even feel stuck by it. Evil is still present because sin, as it turns out, isn't always personal but is, in fact, sometimes quite systemic, outside the orbit of human control. Hell is a place too many of us have experienced during our few short years on earth. At the time of writing this chapter, the war between Israel and Palestine rages on. Governing parties had agreed to a seven-day ceasefire, and the world watched, with bated breath, hoping this would be the final end to an already horrific situation: fighting ceased, prisoners were released, humanitarian assistance reached those most affected in the Gaza Strip. But then the sirens sounded. A rocket had been fired from the enclave. The war resumed.[30]

We may not live in places that have been marked by terror for thousands of years, but we know heartache when we see it. A gulp catches in our throats: we cannot breathe, again. We are struck down by the weight of war, again. But as my friend, theologian and practitioner Kent McDonald says, I sure am more hopeful of Jesus than I am of hell. Be this the case, then it changes the way I see the world, just as it changes the way I cast my steps moving forward.

Call this a filter, a torn-down and put-together-again kind of faith, or just another example of bucking a terrible, horrible, no-good, very bad Greek camp song, but I'm in for seeing things in a new way. I'm in for seeing a little bit of new life burgeon.[31] And if this means shaking up and turning upside-down the ways in which we've always described sin and the subsequent threats we've made about hell along the way, then let the shaking and turning begin anew.

We may still feel like we're stuck on the top of a fifteen-foot fence, but instead of singling out the girl and making her feel like the worst person to have ever graced this earth, we can instead recognize the universality of what it means to be human—she's not the only one who has ever felt stuck, nor is she the only one to feel left shaken by a silly, adolescent decision. Once, when author Anne Lamott was trying to teach children about sin, she took them to the beach. There, beauty and destruction were evident: trash and debris mingled against a backdrop of the Pacific's most poetic scene. Here, we can "admit that the ugly and repulsive and sad do exist, and they are happening, but we don't have to believe it is us, and run away from it, from the cross, from the beach, from our own crooked little hearts. This is how we live with sin, sickness, and a world on fire."[32] Because we humans already belong to one another and to God, we can see the reality of this thing called *sin* and *darkness* and not be left to drown in it. This is real, we might say. This is scary, we might add. But we are not alone: hope is still in this place.

5

Cry Night

Night Five didn't take much of an opener to do the trick. It was Cry Night, after all. We all knew what was coming: conversations with God, alone, out on the wide, expansive field or perhaps with our counselors and our cabinmates. Decisions to follow Jesus and recommitments to follow Jesus and vowed promises to remain true Jesus in the year ahead (or at least until the next year at church camp, when the spiritual calendar started all over again). And tears, lots and lots of tears.

As a speaker, this message was particularly critical. During this talk, all the missing puzzle pieces came together. Campers would finally understand why their villainous scalawag selves needed God to kill his son: Because God loved them! This was the solution! Our golden ticket to heaven lay within Jesus dying on the cross for our sins. But first, I had to point children toward the cross—so I told them the only story I could, a story of a little girl who found herself lost on the streets of London.

"London—now that is a *city*," I probably said in an effort to warm up the crowd. I imagine I talked about the one time I had the chance to visit London, how I relished hearing all those British accents and couldn't get enough of the "Mind the Gap" signs in front of the Tube. I likely dropped the names of some of my favorite authors—Shakespeare and Austen, Dickens and Dahl—monikers that would have made the campers groan when English class was the last thing most of them wanted to think about in the middle of July. These quips only lasted a few minutes before I got to the main story at hand, a story of a little girl who once found herself lost on the streets of London.

I probably wondered out loud whether any campers had ever gotten lost, a nod, a wide-eyed acknowledgment, a hand or two raising upward in response. Then I began to retell the story of someone who also got lost in that faraway place called London. I painted a picture of a darkening cobalt-blue sky, perhaps just like the one we sat under, and of thick fog, rolling in from the banks of the River Thames. I talked about how that little girl must have felt scared to death—scared to not be able to find her way home, scared to not make it back to her family, to her warm and snuggly bed, and to her favorite stuffed animals too.

"In all her wandering, she finally came across a police officer," I would then say to the campers. "'Can I help you, little girl?' the bobby would say in response, and with tears in her eyes and a gulp at the back of her throat, she would finally say the words that changed everything: 'Take me to the cross, sir. If you can take me to the cross, I can find my way home.'" At that point, I would gaze across a sea of faces: Like the marshmallows campers stuffed deep into their mouths during a wild round of Chubby Bunny, the words began to dissolve in their hearts, sinking into dark crevices. We all knew the real clincher was about to come, the sinewy connective tissue tying Jesus and every camper in that place to the pinnacle point of the Christian religion.

Because then I would tell the campers about a place in the center of London called Charing Cross. At a juncture in the epicenter of the city, six different roads meet at a single point; to Londoners, this spot often marks the distance throughout the entire city from which distances are measured. Just as Charing Cross is a landmark, it's also a monument that now hosts a railway station and a shopping district too.[1] "But to one little girl," I likely emphasized one last time, "it was everything. Because if she could find that cross, she could find her way home."[2]

The illustration complete, I tried to wrap up the easiest part of the night with a simple parallel: I reasoned that it wasn't any different for any of us. Because if we could find the cross, we, too, could find our way home. We could find our way to the one who loved us more than anything else. We could find our way to God.

/ / /

What happened next was anyone's guess, but you can generally predict a journey along Romans Road—a violent side of rubbernecking from a couple of chapters in John, viewers were distracted by a bloody, cross-shaped accident on the side of the road. Some camp speakers relished in gory retellings of Jesus's torturous death, reckoning that campers needed to hear the goriest parts of the crucifixion in order to understand how much Jesus truly loved them. I, for one, had a hard time sewing the different elements of the talk together in a way that didn't look like an eight-year-old broke into the Craft Corner at midnight and tried her hand at intricate quilt detailing using a ball of yarn and a fishing crochet hook set left over from the lake excursion in the summer of '89.

But in white evangelicalism, understanding what happened to Jesus on the cross was critical if children and youth were to find their way to God. Within this world, theories abound when it comes to sharing the gospel. There is, for instance, an intricate understanding as to the importance of *feeling* emotions: in order to really get it, you have to *feel* your own sin, for you have to *feel* the suffering of Jesus before you can even have the ability to repent. Like any vigilant camp lifeguard would do, I stood poised and ready to jump into the murky green lake should anything befall a ten-year-old trying their hand at canoeing for the first time. I steadied myself for the night ahead by retelling the story of the little lost girl and then presenting nearly all of the following elements:

- A recap of darkness and of the slimy decrepitude of the human species, thanks to a couple of pluckings from the book of Romans. Bonus: This retelling came with the promise of a new, slime-free, fully forgiven existence, thanks to a little transaction on the cross between Father and Son.
- A bridge. Stick-figure humans always need a bridge to the Big Red Heart (God); otherwise, the chasm between the Big Heart and the stick-figure man becomes too deep and wide, a surefire stumble into hell if you fail to walk across proper support beams.
- A truncated retelling of the twelve stations of the cross. *Jesus was betrayed by his friends. Jesus was sentenced to die. Jesus had to carry a heavy wooden cross up a really tall hill. Jesus was nailed to the cross, one through each hand, one through his feet.* Sometimes a question would be asked after such a declaration: "*Have you ever felt betrayed, camper?*" is an appropriate question to ask children. "*Have you ever had to carry a heavy wooden cross up a really tall hill to die a gory death?*" is probably not.
- A retelling of the Prodigal Son (Luke 15), which is to say, a story about a kid who ran away, spent all

of his father's money on a couple of wild nights in Vegas, got matching "I love Mom" tattoos with an Elvis lookalike, and shacked up with Pigpen when things didn't go his way. Starved by a diet of discarded corncobs and leftover pizza crusts, he realized the error of his ways and took the long way home to his dad's house.

- A dad who forgives his son for getting a tattoo dedicated to Mom and not to him. This Heavenly Father scoops up his children in his love, listens to countless quotations of John 3:16, and croons an angelic version of "Endless Love" by Lionel Richie. Question: Does that make Diana Ross Jesus or the Holy Spirit?
- An invitation to accept this wily love story as your own, along with the specifics of what to say and how to pray so as to receive a golden ticket to heaven.

So complicated was the night's message, it's a miracle campers even made it back to their cabins at the end of the night. After stringing myriad puzzle pieces together, the speaker exited stage right, and campers were left to their own devices—not, to be clear, to their own cell phones or electronic devices (for those were strictly forbidden in the middle of the woods) but to their own thoughts of God, *with* the one human beings have long called *God*. Here, campers were "confronted with the full darkness of human life and with the possibility, through inhabiting that story themselves, of finding a way through."[3] The way through was Jesus on the cross. The way through was forgiveness of sins in a single revolutionary act, "not so that we could sort out abstract ideas, but so that we, having been put right, could become part of God's plan to put his whole world right."[4] The way through was for us and for our salvation by the one who was crucified under Pontius Pilate, who suffered death and was buried.[5]

Make no mistake: as much as I poke fun, as much as I grab the snow globe of church camp off the mantle and shake it a thousand times over until I grow dizzy and those on the receiving end wonder why I can't just drop it already, I still accept this wild story as truth. I still cling to the story told at Christmas of a tiny boy-child born to a teenage girl named Mary and of that same "man who in tenderness, in graciousness, and in sensitivity set a new record for the meaning and the worth of the individual."[6] Try as I might to bring a little levity to a gruesome situation, I am still convinced that a brown-skinned, Middle Eastern Jew died on the cross, walked again three days later, and started a revolution along the way. And when it comes to a very bad, no-good day the Church has long called Good Friday, I don't think there's a more heartbreaking sentence in all of Scripture: "My God, my God, why have you forsaken me?"[7] In that moment, Jesus was alone—far from the love of his father, far from the companionship he'd always known, far from the very source of life itself. Of this verse, author Nadia Bolz-Weber writes, "It is as if the atmosphere, the protective layer between us and the sun, has for a moment disappeared and we are being burned."[8]

When Jesus says this, we, too, feel far from the love of our parent above, far from companionship, far from the source of life itself. The protective layer has disappeared, and the pain singes, sears, burns.

In a single sentence, pain and suffering hauntingly mingle alongside grief and sorrow. They feel more real than ever before. Like a carrot growing in the soil beneath the surface of the earth, our human selves shoulder upward unannounced, pushed out of the ground before we're so much as ready. We feel it in our bones: the weight of the cross and of the God who hung there, all alone. This cannot be denied, not when darkness is ever-present and hope feels nowhere to be found. The light of dawn has not yet peeked over the horizon, but there we are, burning. Are we just not ready to see and feel and experience the light of a rolled-away stone? Because when we are left feeling and remembering and living the violence and despair of this day, the accompanying reality of being human in a messy, hurting, broken world cannot be ignored. We take pulse of our bodies—our weeping, aching, sorrow-struck bodies found stuck in the tension between darkness and light. We lay prostrate in the dark, the respite of closed curtains our only relief. We let the tears fall, crumpled tissues piling on the floor, for the sorrow of this day causes us to tremble, tremble.[9]

/ / /

I write this book as a grown-up, as one who sits not around the campfire, roasting marshmallows and dreaming up new skits for entertainment night, but as a former camper, staff member, and speaker who wonders what to make of a night that too often feels like it went awry. More than any other night, this particular evening tends to go down in the history books of Baptist and Presbyterian, Assemblies of God and Methodist church camps not as one of holy intimacy with darkness and light but as inauthentic and performative, a manipulative deluge of grace. To theologian N. T. Wright, the cross too often becomes the great heaven-and-hell scheme of Western eschatology: "In this view, God hates sinners so much that he is determined to punish them, but Jesus more or less happens to get in the way and takes the death blow on their behalf, so they are somehow spared."[10] Love remains eerily absent from the conversation in this particular interpretation of the cross—even if a hearty quoting of John 3:16 eventually shows up, the verbs become twisted and mangled along the way.

"Look at the two verbs," Wright says. "God so *loved* the world that he *gave* his son. The trouble with the popular version I have described is that it can easily be heard as saying instead, that God so *hated* the world, that he *killed* his only son."[11] Far from an image of God as a loving Father or even a generous Creator, God becomes an angry despot, a jilted lover betrayed seventy-seven times over by the sins of humanity. Even if we try to throw love into the equation, it does not sound like "God did what he did because of 'love.' It's just that it doesn't *look like that* or *sound like that* to anyone trying to make sense of what's just been said,"[12] least of all a twelve-year-old camper sitting in the studio audience.

It sounds instead like fear. In this scenario, Jesus becomes the superhero who steps in to save humanity from the conundrum of a loving God who has no other choice but to send everyone to hell—who subsequently leaves behind a trail of breadcrumbs that leads to the one campers are supposed to want to "get to" in the first place. Fear prompts them into saying yes: they're left with no other choice *but* to accept Jesus, even if they don't understand, even if they feel pressure to make a decision, even if they don't actually believe in the triune God.

But isn't that the point? Within the framework of white evangelicalism, yes, that is the point. If you believe the alternative to accepting the love of God is eternal punishment, lest you eradicate the threat by saying a special prayer and causing the angels to throw a party over you in heaven, then *yes*, seeing numbers tick up on denominational conversion scales matters more than anything else. But when the breath of fear is everywhere, one has to question whether it makes for an authentic encounter with the God of the universe.

I think of the nearly fifty individuals I interviewed over the course of fifteen months: When prompted with the questions *What do you see as problematic or manipulative that you wish you could take back now? What does this make you think about your camp experience in general?* nearly every interviewee responded with similar sentiments—and nearly every sentiment involved a memory of this particular night at camp. Some called it Cry Night, while others referred to it as Serious Night; a couple of former charismatics referred to it as Speak in Tongues night, while a lifelong Presbyterian referred to it as Confession Night. Although part of me wonders if subsequent answers came with the territory of asking such a biased (*objection, Your Honor, leading*) question in the first place, when the experiences of dozens of individuals echo a kindred refrain, you wonder if you're on to something.

"I killed Jesus!" one interviewee remembered thinking to himself on this particular night at camp. Although Jackson grew up in a Southern Baptist home, Christ became real to him in a new way at Windy Gap, a Young Life camp. "Even though I already knew the story of Jesus, it was like I heard it again for the first time. Afterwards, I lay there on the grass, tears streaming down my face. They poured the emotions and imagery on thick. They took me there. As a thirteen-year-old kid, the only thing I could do was say 'yes' because of course I'd say yes: I thought I'd killed Jesus. I *had* to say 'yes.'"

Another interviewee recalled the accompanying dread of the evening, both as a camper and as a camp counselor: "We all knew what was coming. And I know this sounds terrible, but I just wanted to get the whole thing over with. We were church kids. They were church kids. All of us already believed, but there we were, making another decision for Christ." For this person (who wished to remain anonymous) and others like them, it was hard to separate this night from what felt like a curated agenda, which is to say, from the ultimate goal of conversion.

Yet another interviewee, Evelyn, remembered the moment it all changed for her. Decision Night, as she called it, had always been a very moving experience. Her third summer at camp, she recalls opening her eyes at a time when everyone, staff included, was expected to keep their heads bowed and their eyes closed. In this moment, she noticed the camp director counting how many campers raised their hands to make a first-time decision for Jesus and then how many raised their hands to rededicate their lives to Jesus. He jotted those numbers down in a small notebook, which he tucked into the back pocket of his jeans.

/ / /

When Olivia and I lined up an interview during her lunch hour at school, I was eager to connect. As I waited for her to hop on the Zoom call, my mind tumbled down a rabbit hole of memories—of her innate ability to rally the people around her and make others laugh, of the summer she and I crossed paths. I was a twenty-one-year-old lifeguard; six years my senior, she was part of the program team, who led all the programmatic elements of a week at camp. If it was time for the camp-wide beach ball volleyball tournament, Olivia would no doubt be found decked out in a black-and-white referee uniform and blue wig with a whistle around her neck and a wide assortment of witty commentary spewed into the microphone. If the Fourth of July happened to dot the calendar when she was at camp, she didn't hesitate to dress in head-to-toe red, white, and blue spandex, fashion a scrap of Americana fabric around her neck as a cape, and zip line through the dining room while "American Woman" by Lenny Kravitz played in the background. When this same woman, who is certifiably one of the funniest humans I've ever met, took me under her wing, our friendship extended past the superficialities of our outside selves: I got to know the real Olivia, the one who yearned for me to know Jesus in an intimate, personal way, and she, I think, got to know me in turn. We built a friendship that extended beyond the four weeks of camp; we asked the hard questions; we became our most real selves.

"Olivia Lewis!" I declared, my own *Alice in Wonderland* reveries put to rest.

"Why, hello there!" She boomed back with enthusiasm.

Smiles spread wide across both of our faces, I listened as she dove into the conversation: She described her "all-in" personality and classified camp as one of the most formative parts of her faith. Olivia started attending camp when she was eight years old and didn't leave until her late thirties. Except for four summers (when she was instead going on mission trips), camp marked both her calendar and her identity—but it also marked her faith when, as a camper, she accepted Jesus into her heart at least seven years in a row following the "cross talk" at Calvin Crest, a PCA (Presbyterian Church in America) camp:

> Every year you thought, "Oh, I'm gonna do this again," not because I wanted to but because it was like all the forced emotion welled up to the surface,

> and you couldn't *not* accept him into your heart again. When I think about it now, it's like the expectation was that campers would get really emotional. Even if people weren't feeling a particular way about God or about the night as a whole, you knew you had to start pretending to feel that way. So we said yes to Jesus, and we threw our pine cones into the fire, even if we didn't have a reason to pick up a pine cone in the first place.

In this setting, pine cones stood for sin: When a camper threw a pine cone into the fire, they acknowledged, named, and released what they perceived as sin in their lives. But it made me wonder: Did throwing a pine cone also point to giving God control of your life? Did it mean Jesus was in the business of "burning up" all the bad things too? Whatever the symbolism, Olivia remembered how pine cone sessions often started when the camp guitarist began strumming quietly in the background. In later years, she recalled the sessions commencing when someone hit the play button on a portable boom box, the contralto voice of Jennifer Knapp soon filling the air instead. "She just gets ya every time," Olivia said of the Kansas-born musician, whose music topped GMA Dove Awards charts until she burnt out, took nearly a decade off from the public eye, and came out as a lesbian in 2010. "But also, you've stayed up until two every morning. You're hyped up on sugar. How can you not throw your pine cone into the fire and weep at the emotionality of it all?"

I could only nod my head—this night really was deeply impactful for many of us. I remember giving my life to Jesus again, and again, and probably a thousand times again, but I also remember what it felt like to sit on the concrete stairs on the side of the campfire pit and wonder which campers would stay behind to talk to their counselors at the end of the night. The cross is powerful, to say the least: even if, as a summer staffer, you tune out the message when you hear it for the eleventh week in a row, you wake up again when you see the reaction of those campers who are absorbing the message for the very first time—who are, perhaps, encountering the one whose "crucifixion was the day the revolution began."[13] I also remember the weight and the honor I felt when I was asked to deliver this message as a camp speaker: This was a big deal, a huge responsibility. Was I up for the job? Could I put the pieces of the puzzle together in a way that would make sense and invite children to open their hearts to Jesus? When all was said and done, regardless of my words, would any campers stay behind to talk to their counselors and ask Jesus into their hearts? Even if the message might sound different today than it did when I delivered it twenty years ago, Jesus's death on the cross—and the reaction of those who are reminded of this historical event—still packs a punch.

"It's a both/and," Olivia finally said. "I have these wonderful memories. I don't have any regrets. But then, on the flip side of the coin, I look back and go, whether all of that happened on purpose or not. Whether I was one of the campers or the one standing up front with a microphone in my hand, it was kind of a manipulative experience."

My head bobbled up and down in acknowledgment. But then, I couldn't help but wonder, at what point does an experience become manipulative? Does it become manipulative when someone forces it on you or when you start to fake it? Is it still manipulative when you do what's expected of you? These are the questions I find myself asking when two things are true.

/ / /

An interlude of ten-year-old Cara at camp

It was chillier than usual that night at camp. We tied sweatshirts around our waists at the beginning of campfire, wriggling into them by the second or third chorus. Even though we sang my favorite camp song—the one about not being able to get to heaven in a Kleenex box 'cause God don't like them little snots—and wagged our pointer fingers toward the violet sky, just like God would have done to all those crumpled-up tissues, our hand motions weren't enough to take away the bite in the air.

The preacher took his place before the roaring fire, sparks leaping into the night sky. I want to say they shot toward the orange and red clouds hanging on sunset's edge, reaching for the encircling evergreens, grabbing at the ankles of campers who dared sit in the front row. Meanwhile, the preacher man stood at the front of the campfire pit. He gazed across a sea of campers, waited for us to quiet.

When he began to talk, my whole body fixed itself to the fire—eyes glued to waves of orange and red, ears hallowed by the whisper of crackling embers. I stared at the wild man out of the corner of my eye. He was like a bird, arms flapping up and down in rapid succession, jaw crooning upward for a worm. Open and shut, open and shut. "Jesus died on the cross for your sins," he chirped. "The least you can do is repay him with your life." His voice bellowed with excitement, enthusiasm dripping like water from a leaky spout. Our heads bobbed along, echoing *amens* of agreement. This night was important, the special night to get right with God.

Birdman began to quote John 3:16. My lips moved in syncopation to his own: *For God so loved the world that he gave his only begotten son. That whosoever believeth in him shall not perish but shall have eternal life.* In the second grade, I had earned a sticker on the Sunday school chart when I practiced the verse out loud and then a lollipop when I could say it all by myself. Miss Pam had made me promise never to forget those words. If only she could see me now.

I shivered, sitting there in the campfire pit. I wanted the preacher man to finish talking already so we could go back to the lodge for hot chocolate and marshmallows. My shoulders slumped toward the wooden bench in front of me in defeat, head falling to my knees. This night wasn't about me; it wasn't for me. I'd already said yes to Jesus. I'd already walked down the long, carpeted aisle of the little

Baptist church. I'd already been dunked in holy, lukewarm bathwater.

The guitarist began to strum, his song our invitation to do the deed and get right. Still hunched over, I let out a big sigh, relief shaking through my shoulders and back. The night was almost over. We could soon leave. I felt a hand on my back.

"Cara, are you okay?" Peeking through the triangle of light between the side of my arm and leg, I could see the unruly curls of my counselor's hair, the scuffed Nikes she wore on her feet. She leaned forward, shoulders scrunched toward me. Like a mother, her hands caressed my back in comfort. Up and down, circle, circle. Up and down, circle, circle.

"Can you hear me? Cara, are you okay? Do you need to get right with God?" I cocked my head to the side, puzzled. Did she think I was crying? Maybe that's when it hit me: When she saw me lean over and my head refused to unglue itself from my legs, she thought I was having a moment with God. When she saw my body shiver and shake from the cold, she believed the bristling heave of my shaking flesh the remorseful upheaval of a sinner's cry.

Within seconds, the hands of my cabinmates were on me, juvenile hands covering my back and my shoulders, my legs and my head. Hidden beneath a canopy of hair cascading down the front of my forehead, my face remained unseen from the shelter of my limbs. I let another shake erupt from my body. Dramatic shivers ran down my shoulders onto the lowest parts of my back. I shook like I had never shaken before. A dozen tiny hands patted me in reply.

"Cara, it's okay, it's okay," my counselor murmured. "Jesus loves you so, so much." My shoulders heaved again, mimicking earlier motions. I exhaled. I choked back a counterfeit chain of sobs. Squinting through the triplet of light, I saw an audience most captivated by my efforts. They were my pawns, and I the player manipulating their holy outcomes. I continued in my performance, shaking, exhaling, choking back tears. I kept this up until the very end—until we were the last ones in the campfire pit, until I wasn't so cold anymore, until I had the chance to wipe a swath of saliva onto my cheekbones as to look the part of dried and glistening tears.

A month later, the church camp sent my pastor a letter: *Cara accepted Jesus into her heart!* it read. Pastor Jack pulled me aside and asked why I needed to accept Jesus into my heart when he'd baptized me the year before. I merely shrugged, not wanting to disclose the secrets of my fireside performance. Some things were better left unsaid.[14]

/ / /

I think of the word *emotionality* Olivia used to describe this night at camp: when people threw pine cones into the fire, even if they didn't need to throw a pine cone to burn up all that sin, it felt like something bigger was at play. I'd like to call this "something" the Holy Ghost, but there may be more to it than the third person of the trinity swooping a giant hand down from the sky to lob a pine cone from the far reaches of starry skies into a campfire pit.

On the one hand, the word *emotionality* is defined as "the state of being bright and radiant," but on the other hand, its meaning extends to "the quality or state of being emotional or highly emotional."[15] Emotionality, in other words, is the emotional response that happens in any given situation because emotionality acts as a complex reaction pattern, the emotions of a particular person, situation, or experience often building on the emotions of another. Is it no wonder that *emotionality* would become a word used to define the white evangelical church camp experience?

Perhaps I am projecting, but a camper couldn't *not* know there was something different about this night—not when every staff member wore equal expressions of hope and sadness, of joyful expectation and weary resignation about the night ahead. Like a dog that naturally picks up on its master's emotions, campers are not immune to the fact that something is in the air, that there's something different about this night. When sleep is riddled by late-night activities and the daytime hours are filled to the brim with constant activity—when a camper is "hyped up on sugar," as Olivia recalled, and far from the familiarity of their family, the speaker is but a cog in the wheel in a story of emotionality. Add to this a message that takes a child or adolescent from the heights of love to the depths of wretchedness, that maximizes on fear-based black-and-white choices of faith and focuses on the violence Jesus experienced on the cross, all in an effort to define *love.* It's no wonder that at least one person in that room or around that campfire pit would experience a heightened state of emotion—and after that one person experiences such emotionality, that a number of persons would subsequently begin to feel a similar effect, the emotions of one camper building on another and then another and another. Like a giant train of dominoes stacked upright on the sports field in the center of camp, when one falls, you know a hundred more are soon to follow suit. And it's going to be one hell of a mess for the activities director to clean up afterward.

Because it's one thing when something affects an individual, but it's an entirely different thing when a phenomenon known as *groupthink* comes into play. Groupthink happens when all the members of that group—whoever and whatever that group may be—accept and do not question the group consensus. If, in this case, the group consensus is an emotional, tearful reaction to a bloody, violent depiction of Jesus on the cross and to enhancing elements of stirring music or fickle dramatics, then the larger group does not query these heightened emotions. The group plays along. The group seeks to give the people what they want. Have no doubt: I believe God is present in that place, which is to say, in a place like church camp. But I can believe the Spirit hovers over a place like water *and* also believe a spirit of campy peer pressure hovers over a place like the dare to down an entire bottle of Tapatio during the lunchtime hour. *Everybody's doing it.* Further, when scholars define groupthink as "the mode of thinking that persons engage in when concurrence seeking becomes so dominant in a cohesive ingroup that it tends to override realistic appraisal of alternative courses of action,"[16] it's easy to understand how the expected actions of one can become the actions of many. Chris Drew, PhD and creator of The Helpful Professor, goes so far as to say groupthink can lead to "disastrous conclusions because moral and logical thinking is suspended."[17] In this setting, members of a group fail to question the group's competence. Unity becomes the driving force; campers do what the group expects them to do. If the expectation is to cry, then they cry; if the expectation is to repent, then they repent. To confess, then they confess. To speak in tongues, then they speak in tongues. The list goes on, whatever the denominational preference of that particular night at camp: a camper does that which is expected of them when individual thought is sidelined and groupthink becomes the overriding force.

Perhaps it's easy to see how, when groupthink is pervasive, "consensus is manufactured through manipulation of emotion, and the fastest way to achieve that collectively is through widespread fear."[18] A camper fears being sent to hell. A camper fears (what they perceive to be) the wrath of an angry God who killed his own son. A camper fears they killed Jesus themselves. A camper fears they will not continue to experience belonging in the group if they refuse to play along. Because when there is a condition to belonging—if you believe what we are inviting you to believe, then you will experience belonging—and when this condition is what the camp staff subsequently celebrates, acknowledges, and recognizes with high-fives, individual attention, and letters sent home to your pastor alike, then the incentive to belong and to further unify the group only increases.

Of course, this mentality doesn't just happen to campers: it wriggles its way into the minds of camp staff as well. Yes, as the celebrators, the acknowledgers, and the recognizers, staff are on the receiving end of a camper's decision, but they're also the ones who inadvertently carry the weight of those who do *not* make a decision for Christ—who do not, in other words, do what they're supposed to do. Not dissimilar to a timeshare presentation, you go in there thinking you're going to get an easy sixty thousand points added to your account (otherwise known as a five-night stay at an all-inclusive resort on the tropical island of your dreams), but it's a Christmas miracle if your checkbook comes out of there unscathed. You say yes because everybody's doing it. Everybody's going to Maui, to Puerto Vallarta, to the Caribbean Islands. Everybody's raising their hands and answering whether they'd rather golf or shop in their spare time. Everybody's buying it, lock, stock, and barrel. As a camper, if you're in a cabin and eight of your cabinmates stick around after campfire to "get right with God," then you're going to stick around. If *this* is what is most valued by everyone else, then you're going to be there.[19] For young, primarily college-aged camp staff, when the desire for a particular brand of cohesiveness is so big, it's hard not to feel like you failed if a camper doesn't stay behind and talk to you after the big night. If you don't lead someone to Christ, then it's easy to think there must be something wrong with you. Within the framework of white evangelicalism, this night counted more than anything else: if you didn't have a specific story of salvific impact on the pinnacle night of the week, then it was easy to believe you weren't doing what you were supposed to be doing.

How far we've strayed from the truth, from the big idea of how much God loves the world. Far from the gift of a Son, a one and only Son, we've been found curating and manipulating, churning out Little Christs not for the sake of leaning into a revolution but for the sake of boosting numbers on a conversion scale. All pine cones and violent depictions of a bloody Christ and dramatic shivers coursing down the bodies of ten-year-old actresses aside, what could this night look like instead?

/ / /

I return to the story of the little girl lost on the streets of London: as she wandered, she searched for clues that would lead her home. But when she finally admitted defeat, when the lostness of her situation became apparent, she asked to see the cross—because if she could find the cross, then she could find her way home. I still believe the cross of Christ points us toward home, but I also believe that the gospel is bigger than the salvation message alone. The gospel calls for justice, and it calls for wholeness; it calls for the collective redemption of the whole of humanity, and it begs all of us, not just the one, to join the revolution. The gospel extends beyond the personal to the whole of the people. It is not for the salvation of one teeny, tiny camper heart but for the hearts of many, a world made over. The gospel is for the reconciliation of all things—and the cross is but one element of this reconciliation story, one part of this message as a whole.

So we point to the cross, but we also point to the infant who came to earth as a baby. We point to the one who had a mom and a dad and another parent he mostly called Dad. We point to the kid who learned how to be a fisherman and a carpenter, a student of the Torah and a lover of God. We point to the one people called Rabbi and Friend, to the holy man who loved the people around him and offered a place of belonging, without any caveats. We point to the one who offered everyone, including you and me, another way of living—an upside-down God-revolution in the kingdom-come. Just as a whole bunch of people who came before him predicted, this whole story was about the rising and falling that would happen in the name of this Liberator and Prince of Peace. With him came peace and salvation, but in response to him also came violence and resistance. Because the one we point to brought joyful news to some and challenging times to others. But in his life and in his death on the cross and in that wild and holy and crazy thing called the *resurrection* that happened three days later, Jesus challenged the "Roman Empire that offered its own version of peace and reserved it for a select few."[20] For everyone will benefit from this challenge he brings. Everyone can benefit from the salvation he offers, for he is in the business of making all things new.

The cross is then *not* something that causes us to "largely 'thank' Jesus instead of honestly imitating him,"[21] as traditional theories of substitutionary atonement might cause us to do. Because when this is our only response, it only further leads us to "see God as a cold, brutal figure who demands acts of violence before God can love creation."[22] That still entirely misses the point. But if Christianity is an evolving faith, then "the cross cannot be an arbitrary and bloody sacrifice triggered by a sin that was once committed by one man and one woman under a tree between the Tigris and Euphrates rivers."[23] Also, then, Christians, who are "meant to be the visible compassion of God on earth more than 'those who are going to heaven,'"[24] are "invited, not required, to accept and live the cruciform shape of all reality."[25]

Along the way, we become saved by the cross. This happens, Father Richard Rohr writes, even more than we ever realize because "the people who hold the contradictions and resolve them in themselves are the saviors of the world. They are the only real agents of transformation, reconciliation, and newness."[26]

What, then, do we say to children and youth at camp? Perhaps we do still extend an invitation to come and see, every once in a while. Maybe the occasional *thank you* still comes out of our mouths as we remember the one who wipes the slate clean and offers the whole earth forgiveness do-overs. It isn't as sexy as, say, a reenactment of the stations of the cross, complete with toga robes, a fifteen-foot cross, and a cat o' nine tails, but it is perhaps more authentic.

It isn't as traumatizing, nor is it as performative. Far from the reaches of a get-saved mentality, it is without agenda—because it's not about fear, and it's not about the golden ticket to heaven, and it's not about a Son who loves you but the Dad who thinks you're a piece of shit. The hope of the universe doesn't rest on the shoulders of a single camper who asks Jesus into their heart, for the hope of salvation is bigger than an individual camper's decision to say yes to God on Cry Night.

But the hope of salvation is a light that shows up in the darkness, that begs us to cling and search and point to it, even when things get dark again and our squinty eyes can't see a damn thing. It's the light in us and around us, the light whose "promise of hidden, inward transformation is gorgeous hope."[27] Because it's in the ones who become saved by the cross, who then, in holding all the good and bad things of life, also resolve in themselves the rescuers of transformation, reconciliation, and newness they have become along the way.

6

Side Note, Rose Again

If Night Five was filled with heaviness and tears, Night Six brought cotton-candy clouds of levity back to the stage. Sure, the Son of God died a gory death on the cross, but I also got to talk about how he walked out of the grave, zombie strips thrown to the side, three days later. This was the good news! He who died had not been left for dead on the side of Golgotha but had instead floated into the heavenly skies forty days later and was seated to the right of the Big Guy, fifth cumulus cloud to the right.

As a speaker, I first had to paint a picture of life—of life abundant and of a sticky kind of hope that squeezes its way *into* life. As it goes, I often brought us back to the woods, back to the place where life most tends to whisper and scream and shout at me. For years, I told the story of my twenty-five-year-old self who believed it a really good idea to stuff a large backpack to the gills with a sleeping bag, food, water, playing cards, a book, and tent poles. I also tended to believe it an even *better* idea to drive several hundred miles into the forest, strap the pack onto my back, and hike a couple dozen miles, just for the fun of it.

"Some people call all of this nonsense 'backpacking,'" I would often say to the campers. "Other people call it 'crazy-making,' as in 'you're making a whole lot of crazy if you think hanging out in the middle of the woods with lions, and tigers, and bears, oh my, is a good idea.'" I would then go on to tell of an adventure with a friend named Hollie, when we believed it brilliant to pitch our tents in the bear-infested woods of Yosemite Valley.

I recalled how, when it was time for bed, Hollie and I fell asleep quickly enough but were soon awakened by a noise. There was a rustling outside as if something was brushing up against the tent. When I told this story to campers, I made a bristling noise, my hand moving in and out, outlining the shape of a large, rectangular object. I told them about how Hollie and I looked at each other in the dark, shrugging tired shoulders, no sooner returning to sleep.

"But a couple minutes later, we heard another noise. This time, there wasn't just a rustling outside our tent but a breathing, rustling noise outside our tent," I would say, adding in any sound effects I could muster, including the sounds of an unknown, snaggletoothed animal. Eyes wide in anticipation, the campers would lean in to hear the disclosed conversation with Hollie—of discarded pamphlets that warned us about American black bears in the national park and of the flimsy nylon walls that now stood between us and the wild beast. I told them about how we squeezed our eyes shut and prayed a million tiny prayers to Jesus, and God, and the Holy Spirit, too, because we just wanted to live already! But then I would tell them about how the bear wasn't done with us yet. Just as we began praying more prayers to our "dear eight-pound, six-ounce newborn infant Jesus,"[1] the bear started wrestling with another animal, just outside our tent, scratching and pawing and fighting to death. Surely, we would be next, left for dead, the memory of us but a forlorn warning sign at the visitor's center.[2]

At this point, the audience was captivated—thoroughly invested in the story of a real, live bear and of a weird white lady who lived to tell the tale.

"We have to scare the bears off!" Hollie declared, although it could have been me. I told the campers about how we knew what we had to do if there was ever any chance of the two of us making it out alive. Lying prostrate on the ground, as if in a sleeping bag, I showed the audience how she and I raised our fingers in the air. Hearts beating wildly in our chests, we counted down a hearty *three, two, one* . . . no sooner popping up to our knees, sleeping bags falling to the floor.

"Ahhhhhhhhh!!!!!!!!!!" I would reenact, screaming at the top of my lungs, hands clapping wildly at the same time.

"Ahhhhhhhhh!!!!!!!!!" I screamed and yelled and clapped again, and again, and sometimes one more time again.

But it worked, I would tell the campers. The bear left. No longer did it wriggle into the sides of our tent, nor did it try to eat us alive again. Eventually, we fell back asleep and spent two more nights in the woods, just because we could. Because *this* whole experience, this whole tale, well, it was life. And this story of life was, in fact, the entire point of that night's message.

/ / /

Too often, the resurrection of Jesus is glossed over in the typical camp narrative, which tends to focus on the cross. Campers who gave their hearts to a bloody, dead God the night before can now rest assured that the Great Teacher was only dead a teeny, tiny bit—because in the course of history, three days is not all that long. Three days is a long weekend away from school. Three days is Christmas Eve, Christmas Day, and Boxing Day combined. Three days, according to Benjamin Franklin, is the length of time it takes for fish and visitors to smell.[3] And three days was all it took for Jesus to stay dead before he walked out of a cave and started eating dinner with his friends again.

For some who are reading these words, the whole rose-from-the-dead part of the wily story of Christianity has become an afterthought. To these individuals, it is the cross, *and not the resurrection*, that remains central to the Christian story—without the cross, the whole thing topples. In this belief system, the cross is the answer to the problem of sin: Jesus's death on the cross becomes the singular way a human being can get with the God who desperately loves them, the only way the wrong things of the world can be made right again. This is understandable, in theory, if you believe that getting right with God means closing your eyes and saying all the right words and maybe even staying behind in the campfire pit to talk to your counselor—because the whole deal *also* means you officially avoid the fiery pits of hell and gain entrance through the pearly gates of heaven. Like a young boy named Charlie who spends his final pennies on a Wonka Bar for Grandpa Joe, overhears that the fifth ticket winner is a fraudulent scumbag, and unearths the golden ticket to the Willy Wonka Chocolate Factory when he's just around the corner from the newsstand, in the melodrama of personal conversion, the cross of Christ becomes the coveted prize. Everything that happens after the fact becomes secondary.

At this point, it's helpful to point out the significance for evangelicals when it comes to *personally* asking Jesus into your heart. On its own, conversion is "the divinely enabled personal response of individuals to the gospel in which they turn from their sin and themselves (repent) and trust in Jesus as Savior and Lord (believe)."[4] And conversion, in which the individual personally decides to turn away from sin and believe in the forgiveness that happened through Jesus on the cross, is critical if one desires a golden ticket to heaven (or, as conservative theologians are wont to say, an "assurance of salvation"). In this scenario, being saved is all about the afterlife—about where you're going to go after you die—but with the overpersonalization of salvation in white evangelicalism, the whole exchange has become more of a "transaction and has generally been preoccupied with the afterlife and escaping hell."[5] As long as the reward of a future heaven or of the gossamer pearled gates you'll assuredly walk through after you die remains the goal, then humans will always be found chasing after the prize. Sure, you show kindness to your brother on a Sunday morning, but what happens when he cuts in front of you in the all-you-can-eat buffet line after church and scores the last scoop of homemade macaroni and cheese? Or for the camper in our story, what happens when life throws you a punch three days after you get home? You don't get into the middle school you wanted to go to, your best friend shares that she's moving to France, your parents tell you they've decided to separate and will be moving across town from one another. Suddenly, the mountaintop high of loving God and loving other people isn't so easy when the precarity of being human inevitably rears its ugly head. Because when your understanding of faith becomes all about what you can do and what you can get, the onus is also, then, always on you. You become the fish who tries its hardest to swim upstream against the crowded school of first vertebrates—the one who inevitably always tries to swim toward the shiny lure of the celestial kingdom or away from the fearful confines of hell. In all this trying comes the peace of knowing you are loved by God. In all this trying comes the security of having made the right choice. Perhaps it's not hard to see how a kid would continue to ask Jesus into their heart, year after year at camp, when salvation becomes a personal consumer product created for the individual alone. When it's all about you, what else are you supposed to do?

But if death is a beaten enemy, as theologian N. T. Wright says,[6] then God is doing more to transform an unjust world than merely handing over a single admission ticket to the biggest, longest, and most ethereal show of all. And Jesus becomes more than an outdated line from a Depeche Mode song—more than "your own personal Jesus" might dare you to believe about the Christian story.[7]

More than someone to whom you reach out and touch in faith, Jesus becomes "about the work that God is doing in his Kingdom to reorder our lives now."[8] And those who pound down tent pegs of Christianity, further rooting belief into earthen soil, do so because the resurrection of the one who hung on a cross grounds hope itself. As renowned hope theologian Jürgen Moltmann comes to describe, a resurrected tomb-walker named Jesus became the pinnacle point of Christianity because of a "powerful word of promise that stands in contradiction to our past experiences of suffering and death"[9] (including, I would add, the suffering and death of such a man on the cross). We who stake claim to virgin births and three-in-one Gods and men who vie for alone time in the mouth of a whale do so not because Jesus died but because he rose again three days later—because this is how we "move forward in the light of hope toward the transformation of the world God will bring."[10]

I think about standing on stage, telling the bear story (a "bear" I very well know could have also been an opossum, a raccoon, a rat, or even a small, friendly mouse named Stuart Little). I still love that story because it speaks so much to hope. We had hope that if we just stood up in the middle of the night in our underwear and made a whole lot of racket with our hands and mouths, we just might see the light of day. And we did! And here I am now, testifying that I have *seen* the light and that I have hope *because this hope is alive in me.* That very hope is the essence of the Christian faith—the very heart of what it means to believe in the transforming power of a crazy, upside-down story that isn't about where we're going to go when we die but is instead about a dynamic reality that has the power to make a difference in the world today.

Hanging out in the middle of the forest with bears and raccoons and wild camp friends too? Christ is there. Walking home from school on a random Tuesday afternoon? Christ is also there. Desperate for an end to violence in the city that you love, when the bad guys seem to be in charge, and it doesn't feel like there's an end in sight? Christ is there as well. Uncertain whether hope will ever be found in the rubble and the mess of war, when a little town called Bethlehem that once welcomed his tiny, baby body into this world feels closer to chaos than to peace? Christ is there too. Jesus is in these places, not because he stayed dead and bloody on a cross but because he woke up from the deepest of sleeps and rose from the dead three days later.

Like thick slices of bread slathered in butter, glued together with cheddar cheese, and fried on the stove to golden-brown perfection, the cross and the resurrection pair together on the coldest of winter days. Because "to believe means to cross in hope and anticipation the bounds that have been penetrated by the raising of the crucified"[11]—and to believe in this story means to embrace a wild mystery that isn't so black and white but is instead often colored by glorious, mysterious shades of gray. Making the bodily revival of a dead dude the climax of a story is a mystery in and of itself. How do you explain dead as a doorknob, and then wrapped in linens and skipped out of a hillside, and then also will gladly pop back in to say hello except to believe in a mystery bigger than ourselves? Somehow dead things can come back to life. Somehow life comes from death. Somehow it all goes together, and there isn't actually a check-off list of belief systems needed to find a home *in* this place.

But check-off lists of belief systems are easier to swallow, to a certain extent. It's easier to build a faith—or at least a gospel presentation—off the sacrifice of a bloody Jesus, made possible by an angry, wrathful God. Problem: God loves you, but he can't be with you because sin creates a big, fat chasm of separation from him. Answer: Jesus, whose death on the cross created a bridge from God to you. Meaning, now you're forgiven; now God loves you; now you get to be with this version of God forever. *Check, check, check*. Like the black-and-white tiles on the floor of an old-fashioned soda shop, it's not too hard to sit on the counter stool and count the rows, one by one. Within white evangelicalism, one might even say it's easier to focus on the cross because the cross brings with it an expected array of results—and in a camp scenario, children and youth are absolutely going to have a reaction to the story of an innocent man at the hands of a violent mob and an even angrier God. Who wouldn't feel the emotional intensity of this story? Instead of leaning into the power of a God who somehow pumps life back into dead things, we take the road *most* traveled. We give in to box-ticking scenarios of making campers feel bad about themselves because it's easier to speak shame than it is to offer a nuanced story. It's easier to offer emotionality than it is to present uncertainty; it's easier to say yes to the explainable instead of to an unknown mystery that holds more questions than answers and is often overwhelmed by shades of gray instead of the black and white we humans tend to crave. And it's easier to talk about an old rugged cross than it is to home in on holy regurgitations of a man who mostly focused on smaller groups of people after spending three days in the dark—first appearing to a couple of women, later to two men on a long road called Emmaus. In all of those instances and more, his after-resurrection days cultivated a smaller, quieter, more intentional existence.

But the resurrection tends to get less screen time than the cross. It's not as sexy. It's harder to work with. The Holy Spirit—who *had* to have shown up in the midst of flesh-and-bones, third-day revivals—is a squishy sprite, to say the least. So how do you explain their ethereal presence when the earthy story of Jesus's death is just, well, more easily explainable? The truth is that it's easier to work with the cross than it is to work with the resurrection, for the cross is clearly more transactional. Do this; get this. Believe this; receive this. And in a consumeristic society, such as our own, we want clear results. Just as we want to know that 2 + 2 = 4, we want to place our trust in a faith that will produce clear results. *If I believe in Jesus, then everything will be okay. If I believe in the Christian story, then surely my faith will save me. If I give God my heart, then Jesus will well and good fix all of my problems.* Perhaps it's not too hard to see how a transactional kind of faith would come to define an entire people group, further negating the resurrection all over again: It's what we're used to. It's what we know. It's what we buy into and have come to expect on a daily basis, in our churches, in our schools, and in nearly every area of our lives.

Just as the cross is an easier sell than the resurrection, a night that *should* be all about spiritual, wholehearted abundance too often serves as a foil to the ways of capitalism and to a different kind of wallet-driven abundance. New life kicked to the curb, the conversation can easily turn toward transactional, consumeristic conversations of faith.

/ / /

In all honesty, the transactional nature of church camp isn't on the forefront of my mind until I meet with an old pal, Andrew Hoeksema. I first became a fan of his laidback, affable self when he plucked the heartstrings of my friend, Holly, a woman who eventually became his wife. I loved

Andrew because he first loved Holly—but it wasn't until we sat down over the lunch hour that I came to appreciate how his own experiences, both in the church and in camping ministries, gave me a piece of the puzzle I didn't know was missing.

Growing up evangelical in Southern California in the 1990s, camp was a regular part of the calendar year: As a card-carrying member of the CRC (Christian Reformed Church), Andrew remembers long camping weekends with the Cadets, a group whose official title is Calvinist Cadet Corps. A nondenominational youth ministry organization that "provides churches with ministry programs that will enable them to effectively share Christ's love with boys in their church and community,"[12] the group's programs made up the entirety of Andrew's involvement with camping until he began attending youth group retreats and conferences as a high school student. But it wasn't until his first summer of college, when he led a small outdoor program alongside two other counselors for a couple dozen youth, that time seemed to wordlessly expand.

"Our days were super long," Andrew recalled of his first full summer at church camp. "I remember these long days of fun—of canoeing, hiking, horseback riding, playing, and just staring up at the stars at night. But there was this sense of something bigger than ourselves, that we weren't just playing but were actually doing meaningful things together in the outdoors. This is what life was meant to be."

My head bobbed up and down as if pulled, then loosened again, by a string: Tired as we were, days as full as they were, camp made us feel wholly alive. No matter the environment, our days started early and ended late. At one camp, camp "devos" (short for *devotionals*) started promptly at seven in the morning. We trudged down to the campfire pit, schlepping bodies against one another to keep ourselves warm in the cold and foggy Santa Cruz morning. Some of us drank coffee, others hot chocolate, hands warmed by porcelain cups as old as the hills. These morning meetings—during which campers were left to fend for themselves and prepare for the day's activities—often looked the same: a couple of worship songs, a short devotional, a few announcements. On Tuesday mornings, we shared encouragement with one another, hoping, mostly, to hear a camp crush say something nice about us; on Thursday mornings, we shared stories from the biggest night of all: Cry Night, when there was always some spiritual tale to share with the rest of the crew. This early-morning time brought us together and readied us for the day. Tired to the bones though we were, it didn't stop us from believing in something bigger than ourselves—and from wondering if all of this gathering together and sharing life and learning something along the way was how life was meant to be. Because then, we just kept going. We did our jobs, climbing high into the trees and rafting down rivers, fixing up miniature motorbikes and rounding up fallen arrows and steadying our eyes on aqua-colored pool water for afternoon lifeguarding sessions. We did all these things, and we gave them our whole heart, sometimes breaking for lunch and dinner, sometimes stopping to chat with another counselor beneath the willow trees. We worked, and we worked, and we worked, all the way through campfire and club and evening program sessions, tired as all get-out but alive in a way we never felt anywhere else. And we kept this up for four weeks, eight weeks, twelve weeks at a time—our bodies a pummeling force of spiritual desire, desperate to make God proud, determined to hear tales of change and transformation we believed could only happen with the help of Jesus.

But what hooked Andrew as a nineteen-year-old also changed something in him. He told me about how he started working in a Washington, DC, office environment weeks after graduating from college. When the internship ended nearly a year later, a single question tugged at him: "How do I get myself back to camp?" Because church camp held such an innate pull on who he was and on how he wanted to spend his time, he craved a return to sacred playgrounds where Creator kisses creation. Soon enough, Andrew returned to the place that marked belonging for him, which is to say, to the church camp environment. There, he felt right at home, sporting a collection of faded tie-dye T-shirts and webby Chaco sandals, perfect for adventures in both water and woods. There, he started dating Holly, and there, he first noticed the capitalism present both in the Church and in white evangelical camping systems.

Within a capitalistic model, he told me, there is an exchange of goods and services. Theologically, when you stake your tent pegs on a transactional model of God loving human beings only *if* said recipients do X, Y, and Z, then a cash register of religious receipts naturally follows suit.

Think about the ABC (admit, believe, commit) prayer often used as a model for asking Jesus into one's heart:

- Admit that you are a sinner and have made mistakes.
- Believe that Jesus is God's only Son and that He chose to die on a cross for you.
- Commit yourself to a life of following Jesus and serving others.[13]

In this scenario, God can only love a camper *if* they say the prayer. In other words, *if* a camper does what they are supposed to do, *then* they will be guaranteed the love of God (and a golden ticket to heaven) in exchange. So focused on debt and debt relation—on what we humans have to do in order to even the score and make right the deal—we did not believe another way of interaction possible. The whole thing became one theological transaction after another, initiated by the rage and fury of a smarmy pawnshop God—"Til on that cross as Jesus died / The wrath of God was satisfied / For every sin on Him was laid"[14]—and solidified by humans in return. But it doesn't stop there.

"Church is a capitalistic mess," Andrew stated plainly. "We actually consider it legitimate to count conversions. That may not be in the reality of every denomination, but there was always such a focus on 'we just need more people, more people to belong.' And that's still capitalism." Like other interviewees, the more Andrew advanced in both the church and the camping world, the more he got a peek behind the sacred costume closet curtain, so to speak. He watched as camp staff seemed to have a tally counter on hand for everything, including the number of children and youth who committed and recommitted their lives to Christ on a weekly basis. After one stint as a seasonal camp staff employee, Andrew recalls receiving a general email after the summer ended: *In 10 weeks of camp, 103 kids gave their lives to Jesus.* Intended as encouragement (mostly to donors, mind you, whose dollars are often tied to needing to see tangible results, especially if they're going to give in the future), the message made him feel sick to his stomach.

"I am not interested in counting a conversion experience—that's tying faith with numbers. It's like saying, 'Put one in the win column for Jesus!' It's horrible. That's not who God is, and it's not what we're supposed to be buying into either."

"Because Christianity isn't the Great Mall of America, let alone the New York Stock Exchange," I quip. "It's not supposed to be about buying into anything in the first place."

"Exactly!"

Our conversation didn't end there: as the months went by, Andrew and I exchanged occasional texts. I mused over gathering together a few more nerdy theological types to shoot the breeze on capitalism, especially when it came to conversations of churches and camps. Several months later, I found myself on a Zoom call with Caroline Jones, a young mother who spent ten years, first on summer staff and later on year-round, full-time staff, at the Cove Camp in Asheville, North Carolina. During our call, Caroline held her infant daughter while simultaneously directing her toddler son to play trains, to eat a snack, to please give Mama just a couple of minutes to talk with the nice lady on the other side of the screen. Her patience left my nice-lady self breathless with admiration, even if returning to the same, disparate threads of conversation sometimes felt a little bumpy to both of us. Caroline is a former camper—of a camp heavily rooted in evangelicalism, due in part to its affiliation with the Billy Graham Evangelistic Association (BGEA). Originally purchased by the nonprofit to share the vision God had given the Grahams "of a place for people to be spiritually renewed, study the Bible, and be trained to reach the lost for Christ," the training center now leans into being a place of retreat, rest, relaxation, and renewal.[15]

Caroline remembered how campers arrived on a Saturday, mostly so Southern, churchgoing parents could get home in time for the Sunday morning church service. Meanwhile, camp staff didn't waste any time waiting for potential camper conversions, not when an altar time took place on the second day of camp. During this time, campers were invited to go down to the front of the sanctuary and splay their hearts out to God. But the real fun came on the last night of camp when, at Tell It Time, campers were encouraged to tell the whole group a story about what God had done in their lives. Camp staff members, meanwhile, were encouraged to take note of the number of kids in their cabin who made a first-time commitment or rededicated their lives to Christ sometime that week and tell the rest of the staff about it at the closing staff meeting.

"Having high numbers of campers who stood up during Tell It Time meant you might get a little treat from the camp store, usually a candy bar or an ice cream treat. I mean, it wasn't *supposed* to be the only reason counselors nominated each other to get treats, but everyone understood this was part of the reasoning," Caroline recalled. My eyes widened with disbelief: this is next level, at least when it comes to conversations of spiritual capitalism and to practices of a faith defined by numbers. We're not just talking bragging rights for camp counselors who chalked up another tally mark for the kingdom of God—we're talking a *reward system* of bragging rights, complete with the addition of a free, gooey, caramelly, milk chocolate-encased king-sized Snickers bar if you won more souls than everybody else. But holy rewards didn't stop there, at least not for camp staff who hoped to also become the Outback Award winners.

"Wait, what's the Outback Award winner?" I asked Caroline. Not unlike her toddler son, who had now dropped a Thomas the Tank Engine in her lap, eager to play, my question came as an interruption to her thoughts. Desperate to unpack and dislodge the memory, to pick apart the pieces of a memory tied up by insider-speak, I couldn't help but cut in.

"Oh, that person got a twenty-five-dollar gift card to Outback Steakhouse," she replied. "Even if you didn't get it the first week of camp, you still had another week or two to get your conversions up. Quantifiable fruit for Jesus, you know?"

"That is *wild*," I finally said. The two of us paused: I typed her words in full; she attended to the needs of her boy. At the time, Caroline didn't see the award as problematic, probably because she won the certificate a few times herself. But now, nearly half a decade after leaving her position, she feels left with more questions than answers. Just as she wonders how camps are supposed to measure the "fruit" of conversion, she asks why conversion needs to be measured in the first place. For Caroline, the mindset of white evangelical capitalism demands proof: donors, in particular, need to see their dollars at work. And if the proof is in the pudding, then this pudding is a sweet and creamy dessert made real by the number of campers who say yes to Jesus and a nice hunk of change that continues to stir the pot in return.

As time goes on, I continue to dwell on Andrew and Caroline's thoughts: each of them has given words to something I didn't realize was buried within me. For so long, Christianity fit into a snug box of black-and-white thinking. It was a give-and-take way of believing—a buy-this, get-this-in-return type of interacting with the one I called God. Within the camping world, it meant offering my shiniest, loudest, funniest self—not because I always felt that way but because those were the parts of me most rewarded in that environment. It meant learning how to speak into a microphone—how to be a mouthpiece for Jesus and deliver a message that would grab a million little camper hearts, that would take boys and girls from the depths of rolling laughter to the heights of emotional embrace. It meant giving up the need to shower on a regular basis and accepting the millimeter of dirt that covered my calves and my ankles, wedging a home in between the cracks of my toes. Because in all these things, I was giving my all for God: If I could give to God half of what God had first given me, then I would make God proud. Then God would be pleased with me. Then God would love me in return. This transactional way of thinking mattered as long as I believed God was in the business of doing business with me. So I gave my life to this singular path of belief until I couldn't anymore.

When every trail that had led to right and final destinations in the past and when all that giving to and receiving from God in return no longer seemed to land me in the correct place anymore—when it wasn't so much about what I could get and where I could go to see the best view because it wasn't, actually, all about me—I had to leave that place and those people behind. Easy formulas no longer added up. Questions became bigger than answers. God felt more like a snarky mystery than a pithy reply.

I couldn't hold the tension anymore because God wasn't something I could buy.

/ / /

But camp. Camp was something we could buy, if only we had means to pay the price. Perhaps it comes as no surprise that if we dangle consumeristic ideas of heaven to campers—about a future celestial palace in the sky our most devout selves will someday gain entrance to if only we do and say and believe all the right things during our short time on the blue and green globe of a place called earth—then youth and children will reach dirty, grabby hands toward the shiny product offered them. Like a young child who spends all of their allowance on plastic baubles from the dollar-bin section, the satisfaction is immediate and guaranteed. But this contentment is often fleeting, the joy of any new decisions of faith lasting only as long as such a "mountaintop high" can provide. And it doesn't stop there: American consumer culture commodifies everything. When religion becomes something that can be bought and sold, church camp naturally follows suit. We see this in theology, in belief systems, and in appraisals of quantifiable, measurable numbers of salvation—but we also see this in the rising costs of overnight summer camping programs, to the general detriment of underpaid, volunteer, or even paying staff.

Spiritual writer Sara Billups often writes about the consumerism present within American Christian culture. This particular subset easily gains "membership to another club, whether or not we want to belong: the market. The church and the market can't help but collide, often to spectacularly brutal consequences."[16] When it comes to church camp, it's easy for me to assert that the economic model of Christian camping has long been hopping a ride on a train bound for elitist exclusionism. To one interviewee, camp has always been an expensive experience, but now it's become an exclusive reality. What started as a movement to get poor, urban children out of cities and into the woods in the late 1800s turned into a campaign to get mostly white, middle- to upper-class suburban families away from screens and into curated outdoorsy fat farms for a week or two at a time. To another interviewee, camping ministries have moved far from the precepts of loving God and loving other people in a place of nature and now lean toward selling feel-good versions of the Christian faith in perfectly manicured luxury resort experiences.

"Camps that stay rustic aren't doing well," said Evelyn Smith. "When it comes to camp, people want the resort experience with a little bit of religion thrown in there." A camping major in college, Evelyn and her husband have spent the last twenty years working at different Christian camps, mostly in the Midwest. Even though she leans toward smaller, rustic versions of the camping world—because she sees trees and land as an invitation to commune with creation and Creator—she believes camping ministries provide unique places for humans to experience the Divine and each other. But these places, weird and quirky as they are, often remain far from the cultural norms many camps are trying to sell.

"Really, camps need to be bougie? You really need to have spa days for women? If you want a spa day, go to a spa! But they're bringing in massages, spas, facials, you name it." Evelyn laughed, chuckling perhaps at how an irony of indulgence squeezes its way into a place intended for simplicity. "And don't get me wrong, I would love that. It would be great to have a spa day, but how is a spa day camp?" When I think back on our conversation, I recall how her voice began to rise; I could feel the tension of her passion and lament, her desire for what she feels like camping has become and for what she hopes it might look like instead. But is this true across all of white evangelical camping?

I set to find out. After cross-referencing a number of articles, including several boasting titles such as "Best Christian Summer Camps"[17] and "Top Summer Christian Camps for Teens,"[18] alongside articles from *Christianity Today*[19] and *Baptist News Global*,[20] five camps repeatedly showed up as the most popular Christian camps in the United States. Of these five, the price for a middle school student to attend an overnight camp for one week ranges from $1,125 to $2,100, as follows:

- Camp Cho-Yeh, Livingston, Texas: $1,125[21]
- Pine Cove Camp, Flint, Texas: $1,599[22]
- Kanakuk Kamps, Branson, Missouri: $1,600[23]
- Camp Ozark, Mt. Ida, Arkansas: $2,045[24]
- Yosemite Sierra, Bass Lake, California: $2,100[25]

With an average cost of $1,694 per camper, and with one report estimating attendance of more than two million young people at Christian camps in the United States every summer,[26] it's not hard to imagine how camping ministries have become a billion-dollar industry. Even if camps offer reduced tuition for multiple-week stays, fundraise to lower the overall cost, or receive denominational support, one youth pastor from South Bend, Indiana, notes that church camps have had to invest "heavily in their facilities and activities to make themselves more appealing to teenagers. But this stuff isn't free, and as any economist can tell you, the number of consumers willing to pay will always fall when prices rise."[27] The problem hasn't gotten any easier on the other side of the COVID-19 pandemic, especially when summer camps often represent more than half of a camp's annual revenue.[28] For Camp Cho-Yeh, listed above, whose "enrollment ranks in the top 5 percent of summer camps in the US,"[29] nearly 60 percent of its seven-million-dollar budget is brought in during the summer months. Its decision to shut its doors during the height of the pandemic came as a massive financial blow and hampered enrollment for years to come. Even after the summer of 2020, church camps saw decreasing numbers when families couldn't afford the rising costs of camp or were "afraid to send their kids into close quarters where viruses can spread quickly."[30] In the summers that followed, numbers began creeping back up, but camps generally remained well below capacity.[31] In more ways than one, it was a lose-lose situation for the industry—even if questioning mavins such as myself note the paradox of an industry that operates in the name of a Man who chose a path of poverty.

Still, poverty remains a reality for at least one group of people in this scenario: seasonal summer staff workers. For those of us who ventured to dip our college-aged toes in the waters of church camp, we didn't set out to get rich while teaching small children about Jesus and munching on a steady diet of hotdogs and hamburgers—but we also didn't sign up to exhaust ourselves with fifteen-hour workdays and salaries more than 60 percent below the poverty line.[32] As one church camp boasts in its summer staff application, "This is extremely tough work, involving long days and sometimes menial tasks, but it is also extremely rewarding! The eternal impact you will have on the lives of campers, as well as the life-long friendships you will form with fellow staff members makes it all worth it!"[33] Even if the cost of room and board is worth an additional 40 percent, one has to wonder if an average $246 a week[34] paycheck is worth the cost of tough work, long days, and menial tasks—especially if the sum is understood in terms of weekly and hourly rates.

Don't believe me? Consider the daily schedule of a camp counselor:

6:30 a.m.: Wake up
7 a.m.: Staff devotions
8 a.m.: Breakfast
9 a.m.: Morning group meeting
10 a.m.: Activity #1
11 a.m.: Activity #2
12 p.m.: Lunch
1 p.m.: Activity #3
2 p.m.: Free time (with your entire cabin by your side)
4 p.m.: Break
5 p.m.: Counselor meeting
6 p.m.: Dinner
7 p.m.: Evening games
8 p.m.: Campfire!

9 p.m.: S'mores-making
10 p.m.: Lights out[35]

Even if staff receive 24 hours off on the weekends and an additional hour off each weekday, it's not so hard to imagine an 83-hour work week[36]—which equates to a whopping $2.96 an hour, or $41 a day if you base it on a six-day work week.[37] Of course, it could also be said that counselors, who sleep overnight in cabins with their campers, actually work around the clock. Like a caregiver hired for your granny, if something happens in the middle of the night, they're the ones who end up on call. Even if they're asleep, they still have to respond to the needs of multiple campers. Given this scenario, you could say camp counselors actually work closer to 137 hours a week, which evens out to approximately $1.80 an hour. Funny how somehow these pennies become justifiable when (with every exclamation point included) college students are serving Jesus, making an eternal impact, and forming lifelong friendships.

But it doesn't stop there: several church camps cut costs by staffing their properties with volunteers, some of whom go so far as to pay their own way (by raising mission funds) to work at camp for the summer. Fellowship of Christian Athletes regularly staffs its summer sports camps with huddle leaders, camp staff, and volunteers, specifically targeting high school and college-aged students who are "looking for a rewarding and challenging summer ministry opportunity."[38] Several camps recruit former campers to serve as leaders-in-training, staffing menial positions with high school students; in addition to helping with "camper activities and recreation, food service duties, and assisting counselors in cabins," as one camp notes,[39] the volunteer position also requires an application, with references and an additional fee to participate. These worker bees essentially pay to work at church camp for a couple of weeks in the summer.

Young Life, whose 250,000 summer campers attend one of 26 summer camp properties every year,[40] entirely staffs its camps with volunteers. But for a crew of full-time, year-round staff at each property, every position from laundry to maintenance, lifeguards to dishwashers is filled by rotating crews of high school and college-aged staff who donate their time. Full-time Young Life staff (who work for the organization in neighboring towns and cities around the world) leave their homes to serve "on assignment" at these camps for three or four weeks at a time. Because the position at camp is considered part of their job, these individuals continue to receive a paycheck—a paycheck that entirely comes from money raised to fund their salaries, not from the camp property itself. According to nonprofit analyst Anne Paddock, "With nearly $370 million in net assets (of which, nearly $300 million is in real estate), their assets are concentrated in real estate which are virtually debt-free and tax-exempt. Young Life raises about $400 million annually but only spends about $350 million, allowing the organization to pay off debt and grow the general fund."[41] With tens of thousands of volunteers staffing its camps each summer, the quarter of a million campers who flock to their pristine camps do so to the tune—meaning, price—of hundreds of millions of dollars, all of which goes back into its real estate (or camp property) assets. A cycle of capitalism further perpetuates when camp becomes the pinnacle place within the organization to fulfill their mission of "introducing adolescents to Jesus Christ and helping them grow in their faith."[42] Camp becomes the best and brightest place to tell the story of Jesus, but camp, in this context, does not operate unless individuals from Young Life groups in neighboring towns and cities commit to spending a grand or two apiece to get there. As the story goes, the rich get richer, and the poor get poorer, and at least in this capitalistic scenario, the poor remain excluded from meeting God in the woods unless someone sees fit to fork over a boatload of cash on their behalf.

Maybe it's just me, but it seems like we've missed the mark. A collision has occurred between church and market. Its consequences particularly brutal, one has to wonder how we can make right this transaction of wrongs.

/ / /

I return to the story of the bear, which is to say of *life*. This life is newness and restoration; it's new things somehow coming from dead things and waking up to the goodness already around us. It's latching on to second chances, over and over again, and it's popping upright in your sleeping bag in the middle of the night to clap and scream and trust that the big bad bear outside your tent flaps really has left your site, once and for all. In the Christian tradition, latching on to life means pairing the cross and the resurrection together; it means being Easter people in a Good Friday world. But if spiritual communities are to bear witness to resurrection, then, as Erin Jean Warde suggests, "we must be bearers of liberation, participating in creating a world with less injustice."[43] As is often the case, vouching for the resurrection requires that we go through death—because in this extinction, this dying, this end, new life will inevitably emerge.

Is it then wrong to wish death on the consumerism of church camps? Is it bad of me to want to burn any and all transactional musings associated with God in the same proverbial campfire pit that hosts the drippings of a million former marshmallows? When the whole operation feels more like an adventure in profiteering than a chance to gather with Creator and creation in a cathedral hush of nature, then perhaps I do plead for one wild and holy do-over, after all.

The problem is that camps are often locked into systems of capitalism, often through no doing of their own. Just as a chapter that's *supposed* to be about the resurrection and new life has instead morphed its way into false ideas of abundance as a foil to capitalism, this is also *how* the system was set up to succeed. As author Deborah Jian Lee notes, within this system, "the white evangelical worldview is inherently tied to a view of laissez-faire capitalism: economic advancement is perceived as equally available to all and bestowed upon those who worked the hardest."[44] Which church camp wouldn't seek to move toward economic advancement when this is the value most rewarded, in both culture and country? But capitalism is an ever-hungry beast: continue to feed the monster everything it has gorged on in the past, and the gargoyle will continue to ask for more. It will *only* ask for more. The brute will ask for higher attendance and more donation dollars for capital campaign projects; the titan will beg for more yeses in the conversion column, further buoyed by transactional models of theology that make God a mathematical equation of checks and balances.

In *Money and Possessions*, theologian Walter Brueggemann offers a rendering of Scripture that "makes clear that the neighborly common good is the only viable sustainable context for individual well-being."[45] Of Psalm 49, he writes about how the wisdom psalm asks ultimate questions about hope: "The ultimate hope of an acquisitive economy is to get more and to have the most. That ultimate hope, futile in the end, is a great disturber of the common good when the less resourced are left in vulnerability. The ultimate hope in the psalm, by contrast, is that the God of fidelity persists beyond our deathly choices and practices."[46]

We desire better for our camps, which is to say, we want more than bougie spa retreats and counter tickers for Jesus and the complicated mess created by slimy tentacles of capitalism. We don't necessarily want more, nor do we yearn for bigger and better. But we do long for the common good and for a "set-apart space that facilitates relational encounter between the self, the other, and God"[47]—not just for those who can afford its extravagance but for anyone who desires a return to the woods and to the One found in these sacred spaces. Just as the pandemic did for church camps what it did for much of society, forcing a reset button on the system as a whole,[48] what might it look like to hit the home key on additional manifestations of capitalism that have returned to old ways of operating because it's easiest, because it's known, because it's expected? What might it look like to see "every toxic system that interferes and degrades the divinity of . . . every human on the planet dismantled . . . because the bamboozlement of grind culture has been revealed via rest and slowing down"?[49] What might it look like to slow down and *be* in these holy, sacred spaces called *camp*?

The truth is that God is bigger than any if/then statements we humans tend to create: this is what the resurrection offers, if we are willing to make a return to the main thing and to the wildest belief of all. Because the one the Greeks called the Really Real is worth more than a hypothesis, followed by a logical conclusion[50]—for the God a shy seven-year-old me and a zealous, campy twenty-two-year-old me and a hopefully more grounded forty-four-year-old me too. For this is hope and life and revival, all rolled into one.

7

Now Go and Live the (White) Way of Jesus

On Night Seven, the end was finally in sight. Campers would soon go home, and staff would get to rest before the next crew rolled onto the property. Whether that break lasted four hours or twenty-four hours, no one needed to put on a show during that time. No one dared ask anyone else to pull out all the stops. The young ones among us would soon load onto buses and into crowded church vans; some campers would cling to their parents, others to newly minted best friends, sworn irreplaceable. Camp couples (or at least those who had been together since Tuesday afternoon) would inevitably surrender to the sweet sorrow of parting. Scribbling addresses and phone numbers on scraps of paper, typing social media handles and Minecraft gamer tags into newly returned phones, campers said their good-byes and promised to see each other in another year. They swore to meet up at the mall, a park, or sometimes even church. This would not be the end of their friendship, if they could help it.

As a speaker, there was always one last exhortation to give, final words meant to encourage campers in their return home. Although my time on the stage was short, I still had one last tale to tell—a story about journeying toward home, perhaps not unlike our collective experience that week.

I often shared from my childhood, this time of family road trips that took place on extended drives down the I-5 corridor from Oregon to California and then all the way back up again. Sometimes campers heard tales of a biscuit-colored '73 Ford Econoline van, complete with tinted windows, a kitchenette, and a foam and flannel-covered piece of plywood that doubled as both a bed and as a seat for three children. The hoary relic couldn't go over fifty-five on the freeway without an emergency stop on the side of the road to cool the engine, but she came with a thousand memories of a mom and a dad, two sisters, a brother, and occasionally a floppy brown and white Bassett hound named MacGruff the Crime Dog.[1]

"We loved that van because we could grab Cheetos from the cupboard when we got hungry, or we could climb over the back seat and lie down on the bed to nap or read our books," I would often say to the campers. "But we also loved that van because it gave us a story and an experience and memories together as a family. We loved that van because it took us places, and all of those places we visited, well, they changed us along the way. Is it not any different for us and for the journey we've been on this last week?" I could only hope the parallels proved obvious—to the cabinmates who now felt like family and to all the new experiences from the last week at camp. In this final talk, the onus lay on them: "*You* learned something new," I often said. "*You* heard something new because, for many of you, you do not leave here the same person as you were when you arrived seven days ago. But *you* do not journey home alone, for you leave with the God that loves you and the Jesus that died for you. You journey with the power of the Holy Spirit, and you journey with a whole crew of folks, ready to support you on your journey."

By this point, we were all ready for a long winter's nap. It was time for me to get off the stage, to shut my yapper, to stop yammering away. My speech purposefully short, I directed them to get to know God by talking to him every day.[2] I challenged them to pick up their Bibles, to get involved with a church or a youth group, and to keep hanging out with those grown-ups who wanted to see them grow in their faith. I couldn't offer them the moon (or the '73 Ford Econoline van, God rest its junkyard soul, for that matter), but I could offer them a piece of Scripture or two. I could offer them glorious riches (Ephesians 3:16–18), a God who keeps on knocking at the door (Revelation 3:20), and perhaps even one last invitation into newness

(2 Corinthians 5:17). But I couldn't erase the reality of what I was really inviting them into, which is to say, into a place of whiteness that begged them to pull up a chair and stay.

/ / /

Twenty years ago, I would not have said I was inviting anyone into conformity. I also would not have named conversion as the purpose of camp nor would I have identified myself as part of the white evangelical machine. But as Big Mama once said, time has a funny way of changing things.[3] Maybe, instead of starting with purposes of conversion, we start with purposes of love.

"How do you get to love, Mama?" As my friend Liz wrote of a similar phrase, when my younger son asked me this question, I didn't know whether he wanted to know more about "the route to arrive at love, or how it is that we are so lucky as to be allowed to love."[4] He was three or four years old at the time; his words did not come after sitting in pint-sized Sunday school chairs or reading a picture book filled with God stories but during an afternoon spent crouched in the dirt, plucking strawberries at a u-pick farm. As often is the case for him, a question, a thought, an idea will stir around in his brain for weeks at a time, lingering in wait before the rest of the world becomes privy to his inner musings. Just as I'll never know what prompted him to ask the question, I'll also never know what birthed his thought in the first place. Regardless of origin or intent, his question has rumbled around inside me for more than half a decade now, when I, too, am found wondering how we humans forge a path to love. I most often think about what it means to get to love when I'm tired and worn out, beat up by everyday routines of normalcy and repetition, sameness and drudgery. When you're slinging scoops of ice cream into the communal hundred-foot-long trough for the twelfth time in twelve weeks or you're belting out the third verse to "This Little Light of Mine" and you just don't want to wipe camper spit off your face again, even when the whole crew collectively screams to not let Satan *whoo!* it out, how are you supposed to get to love then? I suppose when it comes to conversations of God, getting to love often means recognizing the love that is already around us—the love that is beginning, middle, and end.

Is this what I realized when I finally left, when I no longer found a home in the cozy conformity of the ministry world and of that place called *camp*? The farther I got from that place and those people, and *into* beliefs that resonated with the God I never really stopped wondering about, the more I unearthed a truer version of me and, dare I say, a truer version of God. For me, leaving white evangelicalism behind didn't mean renouncing religion altogether: instead, it meant falling more *in* love with the God who loved me first—because this God made the feasting table wider than ever before. You didn't need to hand over a ticket at the door or give the doorman your coat, but full, free, grace-filled admittance was available to everyone, not because of anything they'd done or would ever do in the future. Getting to love, which is to say, God, was more about noticing the God present all around us, the God who is already everywhere:

God with me, God before me,
God behind me, God within me,
God beneath me, God above me,
God at my right, God at my left.[5]

Because this was also always about the God who was present at church camp, even if we made this God small and got a lot of things wrong along the way.

Sometimes I think about the very last time I spoke at camp, when I jumped at the chance to be back in a place and with a people that felt so wholly, unexplainably *me*—even if an updated or, perhaps, more refined version of me had yet to fully emerge on the other side. I was still the same me, but I wasn't afraid to peer into cracks found in the armor of the Christian faith; I didn't feel the need to hold back from asking hard questions about who's in and who's out, about why we were still doing what we had always been doing. Without so much as realizing it, I had also begun to wake up to who was and wasn't gathered around the proverbial campfire pit with me. I remember looking around the sea of faces seated in the concrete bowels of a stadium seating area. Almost every camper and staff could have worn labels of *white*, *straight*, and *rich*. (Of the last, one can only make this assumption if US standards of living needed to *attend* camp for a week or needed to *not* receive, by way of living wages, in order to work at camp for the summer were any indication.) Where were the people who looked less like me and more like my husband and sons, coated in skin and culture and beauty of Black and brown? Where were the drag queens and the butch lesbians, the gays and the friends whose genders lived beyond the walls of traditional definitions? Where were those who couldn't afford camp, whose parents didn't make enough money to fork over a thousand or two per child per week, or who refused to slap a label of "scholarship recipient" on their kid just for the opportunity to attend church camp? Where was everybody else?

For a while, I thought I had just outgrown camp: sometimes, in all its changing, time has a way of expiring things. Like an old pair of jeans that refuses to play along with the contours of a growing, changing body, I believed our time together had simply run out. I didn't like to sleep on wooden bunkbeds anymore. I'd roasted enough marshmallows to last a lifetime. I'd really liked all those skits about angels and devils and having to choose between the forces of good and evil—because in the skit about two sides of the fence, the devil, as it turns out, also owns the fence, *dun, dun, dun*—but faith no longer felt as easy as a bad skit at church camp made it out to be.[6] In truth, I had begun to poke at presumed walls of conformity, questioning, challenging, and pushing back against expectations of who was in and who was out, particularly within confines of white evangelicalism. According to one definition, conformity is the "*act of matching attitudes*, beliefs, and behaviors to group norms, politics, or being like-minded."[7] Within this sameness, there are specific rules you follow, general guidance shared by individuals that guides the way you interact with others. And *with* this sameness, belonging came when you played by the rules and followed the general guidance: belonging of beliefs and of relationships, belonging of language and of shared understanding of how the world works—or at least of what I thought the world could someday look like if we kept trying our hardest to change our little pocket of the universe.

But belonging, as we've already learned, does not come from anything we do or say along the way. There cannot be a magic formula *to* belonging when belonging has never required any sort of sticky potion or elaborate incantation in the first place. Instead, belonging is a two-way street, a simple fact of what it means to be human in relation to the One who is love. I remember the story of a queer Black man who had not been free to practice his faith in the temple because of his sexual and racial identity. The irony, I suppose, is that the tale of the Ethiopian eunuch[8] was often used to point to conversion: not unlike the entire point of a week at church camp, the dogmatic Lukan tale was often used as an example of what we were *supposed* to do when it came to leading other people to Christ, of prescriptive questions we should ask when it came to creating a potential change of heart. The *we*, in this case, were the right-minded Christians, the ones who followed the general guidelines of those who came before us. As writer Debie Thomas points out, the passage was often promoted as a one-way conversion story of one man (Philip the evangelist) converting another man (an Ethiopian eunuch, a supposed *sinner)* to the Christian tradition. For Debie, "the lesson I took away from the story is that I, too, should share the good news of Jesus as boldly as I can, so that (unacceptable) outsiders might change and become (acceptable) insiders."[9]

Even though Philip takes center stage for much of the passage, the eunuch is equally good at asking questions, mostly, eventually about a man named Jesus. When the two men stumble on some water, the eunuch's question is simple: "What is to prevent me from being baptized?" *And Philip says nothing in response.* Philip says nothing in response because there was nothing for him to say in response: there was nothing to prevent the eunuch from being baptized, from belonging to the God that hovered over these waters:

> I love the resounding silence that follows the eunuch's question. Because silence speaks what words cannot. The silence is thundering, and gorgeous, and seismic, and right. Because the answer to the question *is* silence. The answer—the only answer—is 'nothing.' In the post-resurrection world, in the world where the spirit of God moves where and how she will, drawing all of creation to herself, in the world where the Word lives to defeat death, alienation, isolation, and fear, there is *nothing* to prevent a beloved image-bearer of God from entering into the fullness of Christ's salvation. Nothing whatsoever.[10]

In this story, and in a thousand like it, belonging comes *not* from conformity of belief or customs, attitudes or ways of being, but from gulfs of silence that kick sameness to the curb.

I can only wonder if the same applies to the slapdash walls of white evangelicalism and to the camps it calls its own.

/ / /

True or false, the religion teacher says from the front of the classroom. *Conversion often equates to conformity.* Now, a thousand students may wrestle with the implication of the word *often* in that sentence, because often means *most* of the time, but it doesn't mean *all* of the time. But when it comes to white evangelical church camps, although conversion is not *always* the driving force, it's more often than not *a* driving force—and in the context of true-and-false statements, converting to this particular brand of Christianity also means conforming to matching attitudes, beliefs, and behaviors of the dominant group. It means assimilation to prescribed ways of being in the white evangelical world because this is the most applauded, accepted, *expected* response.

But, then. When the awful conjunction rears its ugly head, a singular question remains: What are we to do with those who *don't* ultimately conform to the standards set before them, including desired conversion within a white evangelical context? If conversion is the ultimate goal (*usually! often!* a student points out from the back of the classroom), what happens when someone refuses to convert and therefore conform to the expected norm? Here, the English teacher formerly known as myself gets to show up in full force. Although I would love to pan a little Shakespearean wit off on you, I'll settle for a good conversation on the merits of church camp instead—which starts with a confession: It was easiest to find straight, white men to interview. It was hardest to find people of color to interview. White women, as well as white queer-identifying folks, came in at a close second and third. Perhaps this has to do with my connections, both in real life and in the online world, or perhaps this is a reflection of the connections of those interviewed (as surveyors were encouraged to pass along or connect me with other potential interviewees). Maybe this has to do with the fact that those who identify as white and straight were also the ones most interested in talking about church camp—not only because they were the ones who worked at and attended those camps as children but also because they were the ones actively deconstructing their faith. They were the ones wrestling with a paradox of feelings about their past and present selves, including past selves who thought church camp was the best thing ever and present selves who didn't know whether they could send their own kid there now. Whatever the reason, I don't want to miss the obvious discrepancy of those who most easily acquiesced to a forty-five-minute interview versus those who weren't "at all interested in reliving the experience of camp," as one acquaintance (of color) kindly said to me.

Because to each of these individuals—both to those who loved every minute of their camp experience and to those for whom camp was a place of trauma—church camp is often touted as a life-changing week. Take the following slogans from popular Christian camps across the country, as an example:

- "Ready for a spectacular week at summer camp? Experience a life-changing summer." (Forrest Home, Forrest Falls, California)[11]
- "The best week of your summer—or maybe your whole year!" (Camp Barakel, Fairview, Michigan)[12]
- "It's not just another week at Lake Champion—a Young Life Camp. This is the best week of your life. #bestweekofyourlife" (Lake Champion, Glen Spey, New York)[13]

As the aforementioned camps advertised, who wouldn't want to have the best week of their life? But one conversation offered me another perspective.

"Are you having a hard time finding people of color because a week at camp wasn't actually how they were expected or supposed to live in the first place? Because it wasn't actually the best week of their lives?" one interviewee memorably asked. As this person (who asked to remain anonymous) went on to espouse, camp staff is conditioned to train people to use the language of *best week ever* or *best week of your life!* But when church camp ultimately asks, invites, and even expects campers of color to assimilate as white, you can't help but wonder if the whole premise was wrong in the first place.

I remember nodding slowly. Their words felt like a sticky glob of molasses slowly trickling down my throat:

I knew this interviewee was right, but this wasn't what I wanted to hear. In the moment, I pushed back. I asked more questions. I thought I understood conformity and assimilation already, if nothing else, because of the research and study that came with previously having written on the subject. A bigger part of me itched to pile on thick and gooey globs of justification, even if I later agreed with everything they had to say. Although I no longer see myself as a cog in the wheel of the white evangelical machine, the privilege of having been ensconced in this world and benefited from this world means I've not fully had to think about the impact of expectations of sameness on people who *aren't* white. Sure, I can look around the campfire pit and notice who's not there. I can throw blanket statements of inclusion around like they're going out of style, but I cannot remove myself from the body I was born in or even from the experiences that make me *me*. And this body, no less, really did experience *best, incredible, life-changing* weeks in the belly of the church camp beast, even if she now sees the beast as fundamentally unfaithful to the Christian message and a causer of deep harm.

But I can seek to listen. And to learn. And to do something with that knowing. Because in this knowing, when conversion too often equates to conformity, conformity to values of whiteness found in white evangelical culture too often act as a betrayal to the beauty of God.

/ / /

The history of camping is one of exclusion rather than inclusion, most notably toward communities of color. In *Sacred Playgrounds*, camping enthusiast and historian Jacob Sorenson writes about how some early private camps could "rightly be characterized as attempts to get white males out of the squalor of city living and domestic feminization to pursue the more manly pursuits of wilderness, self-reliance, and (male) Christian values."[14] Sure, back-to-nature and "fresh air" camping efforts happened as a direct response to the rise of industrialization and urbanization—as cities grew, the need to return *to* nature grew as well. Other reports cite the rise of organized camping as a result of moves out of urban areas: when families were "moving to more rural areas, spending increased time in mountains, on lakes, at the seashore,"[15] a natural desire for "recreational and educational opportunities in these settings quickly grew in popularity."[16]

Regardless of exact origins, these efforts to gather together in the woods took place in the late 1870s. And I don't know about you, but I watched enough reruns of *Little House on the Prairie* to know that white people (including the Ingalls family and their supporting cast of characters) mostly hung out with other white people. Life on the prairie was hard, Indigenous and Black people were bad—or so readers and viewers were led to believe. The North may have won the war, but southern plantations found a loophole through systems of sharecropping, further preventing Black wealth and independence. Additionally, many southern states enacted Black codes, which "required Black people to sign yearly labor contracts"[17] (with consequences for refusal); later, Jim Crow laws, also across the South, further mandated racial segregation. Of course, racial discrimination wasn't limited to a single region or to a single ethnic or racial group, and certainly not, when the Voting Rights Act[18] wasn't passed until 1965, and bans against interracial marriage weren't fully eradicated for another two years. Is it surprising that the camping world echoed back a rather exclusionary story in return?

When it comes to the camping world, soon after the turn of the century, a theory in a popular book called *Adolescence* "gave credence to sending young people to camp so that they could enact their more primitive phase of life."[19] In reality, the theory's ties to human evolution also "fit particularly well with the ideals of white male superiority and inevitable dominance over races deemed more primitive."[20] It didn't stop there: camps continued to co-opt Indigenous traditions and perpetuate racial inferiority well into the twentieth and twenty-first centuries. According to Sorenson, campers lived in teepees. They donned blackface paint.[21] The norms of segregation lent credence to an entire movement "dominated by white children and white camp leaders." Is it any wonder, a century and a half after organized camping got its feet wet, that I, too, would struggle to find interviewees who weren't white when white people have entirely dominated the scene?

The ACA, which offers accreditation and membership for religious and secular camps, boasts more than 3,000 member camps, and serves more than 15,000 members, states that nearly a quarter of its members are religiously affiliated.[22] In a 2020 anonymous member survey, 324 respondents estimated camp staff demographics for Overnight Camp seasonal employees.[23] The findings were as follows:

American Indian or Alaska Native: 0.11%
Asian: 0.64%
Biracial or Multiracial: 1.66%
Black/African American: 2.76%
Caucasian/white: 42.20%
Hispanic/Latinx: 3.03%
Native Hawaiian/Pacific Islander: 0.19%
Other: 0.49%

Now, I am far from a math major, but if you add those numbers up, it produces a grand total of 51.08 percent. Far from a full equation, the ACA notes that "percentages for each segment might not sum to 100% as respondents were asked to estimate the percent in each category but not forced by the survey software to input responses to total 100%."[24] In other words, it's not false to believe that nearly 83 percent of seasonal (summer staff) workers across the camping spectrum *could* be white, if you base the percentage of Caucasian/white respondents against the actual sum of giving respondents. Although one can only hope the guesstimates were either grossly low or completely off base, given the noticeable 48.92 percent gap of missing data, it is not wrong to assume that survey respondents *overestimated* the number of BIPOC employees in an effort to appear more diverse than they actually were. Given that the ACA didn't adopt an official statement of racial integration until 1966 (with a number of camps in North Carolina and Texas subsequently dropping membership), Sorenson summarizes the problem well: "Summer camp became an integral part of the history of white America, but the early exclusion of black Americans caused a tremendous racial divide in camping that is still evident in the twenty-first century."[25]

I'd love to believe the Church a different place, where a beauty of diversity becomes the cornerstone of belief in God. Just as God is not male, God is not white. But at church camp, when a white camper asks a camper of color, "Are you on scholarship here?" or when a Black counselor is asked, "Does your family ever run out of food stamps?" racism persists.[26] No matter how true and real and pure the gospel, camp itself remains a place of hate and trauma—and the longer camp remains unsafe for children of color, the longer it remains a haven for a majority white population. Even though the US Census Bureau projected that nonwhites would account for the majority of the nation's seventy-four million children by 2020 (with whites dropping below 50 percent of the population by 2045),[27] almost 70 percent of ACA "camps reported that 70% of their kids were white, non-Hispanic"-identifying.[28] For Anthea Butler, author of *White Evangelical Racism*, the problem is obvious when "'Christian race,' America, and belief" become synonymous with one another, and the conflation of these three identifiers "causes evangelicals to ignore their racism."[29] Because they believe Christianity an all-encompassing identity and a race in and of itself, "when some evangelicals say they don't see color, they really mean it. They just see whiteness. No color but the dominant one."[30] As the story too often goes, this plays out in a church camp context when anything *outside* of the bounds of whiteness shows up on the property. Campers and staff of color are questioned, labeled *different*. In this scenario, they are often othered because *they* do not fit what dominant white evangelical culture believes a Christian should look like in the first place.

In my research, I came across a blog post written by a young Black woman named Danaya. It starts with the following (powdered) quote: "'Camp is for black kids.'—No one ever."[31] A former veteran staff member for Camp in the Community, one of five camping ministries of Holden Conference Camping,[32] Danaya quickly lets the reader know that summer camp is actually *not* for Black kids:

> Any black kid I saw, I wanted them to be my camper because I knew that their white camp counselors would have no idea what they were going through. I remember being asked if I were in romantic relationships with the other black staff members simply because we were black. I remember campers thinking that my black campers were my children or otherwise related to me. I remember being asked if I was related to Frederick Douglass and Rosa

> Parks because these were the only Black people that my white campers could recall off the top of their heads. I remember being told by an 8-year-old camper that I needed to die because I was black. I remember one of my black campers being humiliated in the bathrooms because she didn't wash her hair every day. I remember campers asking me if I ever took a shower because I was so brown, I looked dirty all the time.[33]

My eyes filled with tears when I read Danaya's words, the weight of her insights heavy within me. This stranger speaks to truths only she can, for hers is a real, knowing, lived experience—an experience no camper or summer staff member should ever have to go through but a reality she lived, day in and day out. The real clincher came with this realization: "I remember thinking that, though I loved my kids and the staff and I loved being able to experience God in His creation, summer camp could not be a place for me, a black kid."[34]

The story isn't all that different for Reverend Mitchell Felton, an Episcopal youth minister in Washington, DC, and a self-described Black kid from a working-class family in rural South Carolina. Much of Mitchell's formation as a Christian was informed by white evangelical subculture, so much so that he found he couldn't be a Christian in certain environments unless he adopted specific elements of the culture. As formidable as these experiences were to his development, he couldn't escape the racism and classism deeply embedded within these organizations. Conned by the cultural and theological assimilation he experienced without so much as knowing it, his list of lamentations is long, and rightfully so:

> I lament the idea I needed to buy Chacos, use multi-color highlighters for my Bible, and listen to white Christian music to feel like I was a part of what God was doing. As a Black kid, I felt forced to sacrifice the parts of my blackness I loved and the parts I didn't even know existed to have a seat at a table which was built on white normativity. I do not like Comfort Colors shirts, but that's what I wore, because Young Life told me that's what I should like. My blackness was once used as the punchline of a skit, because my Area Director said, "There would be nothing funnier than a large, angry, Black man coming in and tackling someone!"[35]

In a culture permeated by values of whiteness, when Mitchell later came out as bisexual, his "raft of Black dignity could no longer handle the milky tsunami" of white evangelicalism, and he began to drown in a "bottomless, salty sea of whiteness, with no lifeboat in sight."[36] The young man felt like he was drowning in a culture that never intended for him to succeed. Although Mitchell later found refuge in the Episcopal tradition, the racism embedded within the church camp world continued to rear its ugly head.

When the two of us were able to steal half an hour of time together, I was bowled over by his genuine kindness and warmth. His smile is so wide, his teeth sparkle. He belongs on a Colgate commercial, showcased beyond a computer screen in the middle of the day. Really, I want to know him. I want our friendship to extend beyond singular conversations of a place called *church camp*. On our call, Mitchell told me about the summer he was invited to be the chaplain at Camp Kanuga, a camp in the Blue Ridge Mountains of western North Carolina "committed to fostering an environment of connection to Creation, the Creator, Community, and Camper within all who come through the gates."[37] The property is shared by Camp Bob, a camp of the same denomination that envisions a "safe and supportive environment where campers can be themselves."[38] Although the two camps occupy the same forested land, they serve two distinct populations: Kanuga caters to predominately white, middle-to-upper-class campers, while Bob serves low-income kids of color.

In his role as the chaplain, Mitchell would often need to go to the front office to make copies or retrieve different items. He recalls how one particular type of conversation happened numerous times:

"Hi! I'm the chaplain for Camp Kanuga," he would say.

"Oh, you mean Camp Bob?"

"No, I mean Kanuga," he would clarify, time and time again. To some of their staff, a Black person could not be a staff person at Kanuga, let alone serve as camp speaker for the summer. I shook my head, anger pushing its way through to my fingertips. I couldn't type fast enough.

Part of me wishes both Mitchell's and Danaya's stories were uncommon, siloed experiences. I wish I could take away their pain: even more, I wish trauma and church camp would have never paired together in the first place. But I also know they are far from alone in their stories. Interviewees recalled camp properties interrupting "regular" (read: mostly white, from suburban areas) weeks at church camp for an "urban" (read: Black and brown, from urban cities) week at camp. "A separate week was created for them, *for their kind*," one interviewee remembered overhearing at a staff meeting. "But there was this disconnect: it was like the whole thing was blamed on race, culture, or ethnicity because all the white staff didn't know how these parts of identity might also be a part of faith." Others still told stories of Black staff members whose nicknames often came from Black television characters, sports figures, or personalities: "Fresh Prince," "Michael Jordan," and "Oprah" became legends at their respective camps, the lone Black staff member for the summer a celebrity in their own right. Meanwhile, white staff members adopted names from a variety of sources. "If someone dubbed them 'Tomahawk,' they got named Tomahawk," one former summer staffer replied. "But white people were also named 'Aunt Jemima,' 'Froggy,' and 'Gringo'—it didn't matter. They got to be whoever they wanted to be, going by names that were racist or derogatory or just plain wrong. They got to do it because they ruled the place."[39]

I am also reminded of Katie Carper, a certified life coach, writer, and advocate. For Katie, a white adoptive mother of a Black-white biracial boy with Down syndrome and autism, her frustration in trying to find more inclusive camp spaces has only deepened over time. As a camping major at Cairn University outside of Philadelphia, after meeting her husband during a summer internship at a conservative Christian camp in Philadelphia, the two have worked in full-time Christian camping environments for their entire adult lives. As well versed as Katie is in the camping world, she struggles to find answers to a myriad of questions, both for her son and for thousands of kids like him.

"Who is camp really for?" she asks. "The able-bodied? Neurotypical? Are we segregating camps, like we have with our schools? Are camps just representative of the culture, and if so, which culture? Is there space for my son and for kids like him and for the physically disabled? Does he have to go to a special camp, reserved only for kids like him? If not, what do full-inclusion camps look like?" Katie asks the questions all of us should be asking, the holy fire within her a match I can only hope will not burn out anytime soon.

The reality is that church camps can try to spin their data to paint a prettier picture, but sacred playgrounds of white evangelical camping ministries remain largely inhospitable to people of color, as well as to those who do not fit a mold of white and able-bodied. It's not, then, about including pictures of children or staff of color on promotional websites, nor is it about advertising that camp is going to be the *best, incredible, most life-changing* week for everyone who passes through its gates. Because it's not. As long as we continue to preach a message of assimilation and conformity—that there is one right culture within this one narrow swath of Christianity to which one can belong and be defined by, therefore leaving behind all previous notions of faith and identity—then this is a false white gospel. Then we have and are and will continue to get this message wrong.

/ / /

I return to a story of an old Ford Econoline van and to bits and pieces of a family road trip. If the analogy paired correctly, then campers could see the connection from a road trip down the I-5 corridor and back up again to seven days at a holy and magical place called *camp*. They could connect the dots between a mom and a dad, two sisters, a brother, and an old hound dog named MacGruff to fellow travelers that week: their cabinmates, their counselor, other campers, the entire camp staff. And they could know that the "road trip" in that place where God and nature kiss was soon going to come to a close—that when they returned home to a place where it wasn't as easy to love God and feel loved *by* God in return, there were still things they could do to bring back that mountaintop high, to feel like they had returned again.

But we also learned that leaving a place geared toward conversion means ascribing to invitations of conformity and assimilation. It results in a beggary toward whiteness and exclusion to those who aren't white, who do not fit an aesthetic mold of peach-colored skin or play by the rules of white evangelicalism. For many Black and brown campers and staff people, it means quite the opposite of a *best, incredible, life-changing* week. Church camp can instead mean a living hell. What, then, does it mean to swing wide the gates of these sacred playgrounds, as Jacob Sorenson dubs them, so every single human can encounter the One who sits at the center of it all?[40]

I'd like to think it starts with remembering our shared humanity and with the simple act of honoring one another as we are, which includes *who* we already are. As a minister, there is no greater a message I can preach on a Sunday morning than a reminder of the sameness that knits us together: *You are loved simply because you are human. You matter simply because you are a child of God.* In this loving and this mattering, everyone is welcome to the table—everyone is welcome to this place because we share in common a bond of fleshy humanness. When it comes to the conversation at hand, I wonder if this is where we start as we start all over again. Victoria Loorz, author of *Church of the Wild*, says it like this: "The idea of a divine indwelling at the center of the whole universe, with every unique part in conversation with the others, has many names. What Thich Nhat Hanh names the *web of interning* is aligned with what Robin Wall Kimmerer calls *sacred reciprocity*. David Whyte calls it the *conversational nature of reality*, and quantum scientist David Bohm uses the term *implicate order*. Martin Luther King Jr. called it an *inescapable network of mutuality*, which he said was 'tied in a single garment of destiny. Whatever affects one directly, affects all directly.'"[41]

Knit together by the thing we most share in common, "I am because *we* are," or "I am because *you* are."[42] When we cling to *ubuntu*, a belief in the universal bond of sharing that connects all humanity, coined by former archbishop Desmond Tutu—then just as my joy becomes your joy, my pain becomes your pain as well. If, in this situation, some of our human family cries out for experiences far from good and beautiful and pure, as we desire might happen at camp, then we listen. In a camping scenario, those who have long held positions of power, which often include white, able-bodied individuals, listen to those who have been marginalized at the *hands* of the powerholders. We bring changes to these holy places because we can't afford to let hate and discrimination continue to fester like gaping wounds to those with whom we share a bond. As Danaya's blog post declares, "You should not have to be wealthy and white to go to summer camp or learn about God, nature, your community, and the environment. You should not have to be wealthy and white to learn that your life has value and meaning and that you are loved, important and deserving of all the good and beautiful things that life has to offer. And more importantly, you should not have to be wealthy and white to make a s'more."[43]

This is, of course, but a start. When church camps have not historically been a safe place for communities of color, what does it mean to create safety? What does it mean to embody environments where every camper thrives, where a diversity of beauty is not merely represented but celebrated in fullness? And in this particular context, are affinity camps the way to go, or is it more so a matter of doing the deep and necessary work true justice requires? I think of Rescue, Release, and Restore (RRR), an organization located in the heart of Chicago's South Side committed to "transforming self-worth and empowering youth through leadership training, artistic expression, and mentorship."[44] What began as a camp program called SIMBA (Safe in My Brother's Arms) for Black boys aged 8–17 soon grew to include a program called SIMSA (Safe in My Sister's Arms) for similarly aged Black girls; eventually, RRR added a third program focused on multicultural youth leadership offerings for teens of all different racial backgrounds and operates single-week programs at rural camp properties throughout the Midwest. In a similar vein, I remember Camp Be'chol Lashon, which finds a home in the emerald, rolling hills of California's Marin County. According to its founders, "It's the only sleepaway summer camp specifically serving Jewish children of color, creating a safe space for candid conversations on race and identity."[45] The camp runs for two weeks every summer, mostly serving campers from Northern California, as well as from Texas, Montana, and New Jersey.[46] And then there's Bridge Builders, a one-week camp at Living Water Ministries in New Era, Michigan, that believes real change happens in the lives of young people who explore systemic racism in the faith-formative community of camp.[47]

For Aisea Taimani, a creative artist and musician at the ELCA-affiliated camp for the past five summers, Bridge Builders shows a diverse group of high school-aged campers a different way forward: "There's so much we're missing out on during a typical week at camp. We create brave spaces to process grief, forgetting also that joy comes from grief. But these students learn how to suffer together, grieving alongside our siblings that experience being and living in this world as people of color." For Aisea, a Tongan man from the San Francisco Bay Area, the need to create space, tell the truth, and honor pain is imperative if real change is going to happen. Without it, camps merely lend a good talk, slapping Band-Aids on deeper issues of racial injustice in faith-based spaces.

In truth, there is no easy answer, no perfect solution to the aforementioned questions. The both/and nature of my conversation with Aisea confirms this: affinity camps intentionally serving campers of color are necessary to the church camp world. But so are camps that primarily cater to white campers—*if* they can commit to digging in and doing the work necessary to address systemic discord. Right now, it doesn't seem like either is prioritized within camping ministries. When multiple searches for church camps serving children of color, run by staff of color, continued to draw a void for me, I took to Instagram Threads. "You're not going to find that in the Christian camping world," one acquaintance stated. "It's just not in the cards," another respondent added. "I just don't trust them." For the latter, a Black woman, sending her kids to sleepover camp would never happen because of the cultural differences inherent in raising children. For her and her immediate community, a weeklong stay at an overnight camp is a moot point, a non-conversation.

As for me, it's easy to want to tie up centuries of oppression, discrimination, and hate with neat and tidy bows of honor and celebration. In an effort to esteem racial, ethnic, and cultural differences, I can easily gloss over nuanced conversations, the ignorance of my *learned* experiences of race incongruent with any *lived* experiences of race. Let us call out the beauty present in all the different shades found in a box of skin-tone-shaded color crayons, I want to say. Let us celebrate the rich array of human beings to cross camp's path! Let us make right hundreds of years of too many wrongs so, together, we can hold hands and walk under holy arches of camp! Try this approach, and we're left singing endless rounds of "Kumbaya" on a plucky camp guitar—the harmony 'round the old campfire might sound next level under a dazzling azure and salmon sky, but we have, once again, missed the point.

Instead, perhaps we lean into a different kind of honoring, an honoring that centers itself on love. A woman named Sumiko comes to mind. One of the first people I interviewed, after nearly four decades in the SBC, Sumiko left the denomination to find a version of God that wasn't white and wasn't male. She yearned for a God that was perhaps a little more like her, an Asian woman. Camp had long been a part of Sumiko's world as a child, as a summer staff member, and, later, as a youth pastor. Years went by, but as luck would have it, she found herself back on the grounds of the same SBC camp. She recalled walking along the grounds, the entire place empty, as campers had already left for the summer.

Here, God met her in the woods.

Sumiko, God looks like you.

What do you mean? Even though Sumiko knew she was made in God's image, an image of a white, male God still lived in her mind.

No, God looks like you.

For Sumiko, "a 4'11" woman Asian youth pastor," as she describes herself, a new journey began under a canopy of Ponderosa Pines that day. A voice of beauty and compassion, wholly uninterested in conformity or sameness or ways of whiteness, met her in love.

I can only hope for the same in all the sacred playgrounds we call home.

Epilogue

A month before the first draft of the book was due, I holed up in a basement guest room of my friends Jana and Peter—easily two of the most amiable humans I've ever known. When I knocked on the door of their eight-hundred-square-foot cabin in the woods, I immediately felt at home. I cozied under a blanket on their big brown couch and felt enveloped by two people who love and accept me exactly as I am. Mostly, though, I was there to write. I finished long sections of the book; I walked Libby the dog on winding trails dotted with the slime of banana slugs; I saw the faces of people I've known for twenty-five years, the faces of people who still love me even if they wonder whether I just want to burn it all down.

It, of course, is *camp*. It's that same marigold pamphlet of a camp I discovered in the career center as a freshman in college. It's the place I worked for four summers in college, where I later became a camp speaker and musician in the decades to follow. I do not lie when I say I feel most at home in this place because it's not just Jana and Peter who warm me with hospitality, but it's camp, the very place that started it all.

When the three of us sat on the couch, sipping our coffee and tea, we talked about camp. I thought about all the stuff that has accompanied my faith: heaven and hell, angels and devils, and all that sin that supposedly lived inside you that can't be remedied but for the cross. I thought about how normal it all was—how I didn't question the many facets and beliefs that accompanied white evangelicalism because that's just the way it was. That's just what believing was.

"I knew I could never work as a camp counselor again when they brought out a skit about an angel and a devil and all that sin that lives inside us. I think it was meant to inspire us to choose heaven over hell, but it did the opposite for me." Jana took a sip of her tea as she recalled the single summer she spent working as a counselor at church camp.

"What did it do for you?" I asked.

"Well, it made me never want to be a part of that kind of God, that kind of Christianity. I was nineteen years old, but I knew enough to know I didn't want to be a part of it." Although Jana later worked as a lifeguard and in the snack bar, she chose to work in support roles so as to not have to encourage campers to fall in line with that kind of thinking. I took in her words, mulling them over.

Our experiences were so different and yet so similar in other ways. She may have evolved in her understanding of sin and hell long before I ever caught on, but that's not really what matters. What matters here is what we share, and what we share in common is a little place called *church camp.*

/ / /

When the three of us each went our separate ways, to our respective areas of work, I kept thinking about what it means to return to a place and a people so formative in my faith journey, so critical to my personal identity. I am not the same person I was when I first stepped onto the grounds of camp or even when I kept coming back for more, five, ten, fifteen years later.

Libby became my respite at odd hours throughout the day. *Want to go on another walk, Libby? Want to go explore, Libby?* We do not venture to anything I've not explored a thousand times before. The hills are harder on my knees, but the bay laurels and the Douglas firs, the willow trees up at the top of the property and the redwoods down below are all the same. The eleven-mile-an-hour signs are the same. The Wagon Wheel and the campfire pit and the zip line where I dressed in Americana red, white, and blue and threw watermelons to the ground while Lenny Kravitz's

"American Woman" played in the background are all the same too.

As Libby and I stood in that place, surrounded by a tower of trees, swallowed up by different shades of green and brown and gray, I thought of a song we sang to campers each night before they went to bed:

May the Lord, mighty God,
Bless and keep you forever.
Give you peace, perfect peace,
Courage in every endeavor.
Lift up your eyes and see His face,
Filled with grace and love.
May the Lord, mighty God
Bless and keep you forever.

The same God I met as a summer staffer in 1998 was still there. That same God was still in me, for that same God was still present in that place. Maybe the truth is this: even if and when and as we change, even as we evolve and tear down and reconstruct new versions of faith, we are found enveloped in a Mystery who meets us in that place, who looks over us with grace and love.

Even if this God now sings a more nongendered version of the song, this same God still sings a goodnight prayer over each one of us. Even if we are sometimes left with more questions than answers, we remember the wild sameness of God—of a God who was always so much more expansive and inclusive and welcoming than we could have ever imagined. Even when, even if, we once fully found ourselves invested in rules of white evangelicalism, the God that was there, in those places called *camp* twenty-five years ago, is the same God that's in the places we call *camp* today.[1]

/ / /

"Is this a book about church camp or a book about faith deconstruction?" an early reader asked me.

"Yes," I replied, a lopsided grin reaching toward my left cheekbone. I may not have been asked a yes-or-no question, but sometimes a demonstrative *yes* is the only thing you can say in response. When my family recently sat around the dinner table with my aunt and uncle, my younger son asked a question of the six of us gathered there: *Would you rather have a unicorn horn or a monkey tail?* It's a valid question. I, for one, lean toward the magic of a sparkly rainbow horn poking out from the middle of my forehead, even if there is something to be said about balance and agility and swinging from branches in your spare time. *Yes*, Uncle Chris declared. Why limit the charm of a single appendage when both imaginary options are valid in and of themselves?

Maybe the same goes for this book. My own deconstruction experience, if we have to call it that, would not have happened without a place called *church camp*. To me, the word *deconstruction* doesn't seem to fit, though, at least not when it comes to matters of faith. It feels overused, too broad of an identifier for each one of our very different stories. Often thought of as a phenomenon within American evangelical culture, those who deconstruct their faith often tear the whole thing down to the ground. They rethink previously held belief systems, often to the point of no longer identifying as Christians anymore. However, my experience of leaving church camp, and eventually of leaving white evangelicalism, didn't happen because I actually tried to *think* my way out of any previously held beliefs. The whole thing felt less like I was part of a phenomenon and more like I was on a slow-moving ship bound for dormancy, even if the phenomenon at hand was actually a part of greater twenty-first-century religious trends. Like a beekeeper who tries to move a beehive from the front yard to the backyard, I couldn't move my hive of religiosity more than three feet at a time, not if I wanted to keep the hive intact and prevent all those little worker bees from getting confused and returning to the original location. My faith was a slow-moving beast if there ever was one (even if the analogy does make me wonder whether I'm the queen bee, the worker bee, or the blessed hive of my own story).

Instead, my experience of walking away from church camp felt more like a spiritual evolution or perhaps even like a becoming. But of this becoming, God hadn't changed all that much.

I remember my conversation with Sumiko, the Asian woman God spoke to in the woods. When she returned to the camp of her youth and much of her adulthood, only one thing was really true: "The God that I met there is still the same God. Yes, the theology and all the stuff is fluff around it, but something about camp and the mystery of camp, and meeting God there, is beyond words."

I remember how Sumiko's eyes pooled with tears as she told me this story. The very place that hurt her, whose people didn't always know what to do with her presence and her personhood, began to pour out oil like a healing balm. The God of this place had been in her all along—that part hadn't changed, even if it felt like no other part of her faith had stayed the same.

Outsiders may question the changes evident in Sumiko's life: she refers to God by female pronouns; she attends a church that centers the healing, wholeness, and flourishing of women of color; and she continues to embrace an image of God that looks more like her than like the white male God she was trained to see. All of these relics are perfectly fine under the umbrella of acceptable things to believe about the One we humans called *God*—but a smile crosses my face when I remember that the same God who met Sumiko as a Southern Baptist is the same God that meets her in the Divine Feminine today.

As Libby and I walk down the hill from camp, my knees don't feel quite so wobbly anymore. Downhill helps, I suppose. When we come across a mossy embankment, she stops and sniffs the ground. Fallen branches and twigs, pine needles and tufts of grass have provided her with her quite an assortment of smells, I'm sure. I pick up a branch. I stare at the emerald-colored wall. Then, carving as best I can into moss and dirt, I write three words: *I [heart] camp.*

Acknowledgments

Erin Lane and Micha Boyett, this book would not be a reality had the two of you not stood in the gap with me. Erin, you were the one first to identify that sticky throughline of camp; Micha, your insight was crucial in helping me dig heels into an experience you innately understood. Both of your fingerprints are on every page of this tale. I cannot thank you enough.

To David Morris, Agent Extraordinaire: that's how your name appears on my cell phone, maybe, mostly because it's true. Thank you for believing in my words from the very start and for listening attentively to each and every one of my ranty emails and phone calls.

A huge thank-you to Ranada Young, Jessica Floyd, Kurt Kroon, Erin Straza, Irene Plunkett, Marlene Hekkert, Peter and Jana Thomsen, Jeremiah Fair, Melisa Bass, Neidy Hess, Annie Rim, Catherine McNiel, Kris Gromm, Liz Ditty, Mindy Haidle, Sarah Lemley, and other sojourners along the way. You were more than generous conversation partners to me: Thank you for helping me wrestle and wriggle my way through muddled thoughts and sometimes even offering me a bed and a quiet space to figure it all out. I am so grateful to each one of you.

Thank you to my extended writing community: Lauren Winner, Amy Peterson, and Charlotte Donlon, I am grateful for your initial feedback during Craft and Revision. Kelley Nikondeha and Ashley Hales, thank you for being in the daily grind of the writerly (Voxerly) life. Liz Tichenor, I'll gladly share a writing weekend with you anytime and promise not to say a single word—except for meals and walks around the camp property. Then you won't be able to shut me up.

This book would not be a book without the generosity of those individuals who shared their insights and experiences with me. Thank you to the following folks whose stories dot the pages of *Church Camp:* Kristin Wolven, Jamie Van Nuys, Sumiko Wong, Holly Hoeksema, Kim Cooper, Katie Carper, Mark Wagner, Jen Etter, Billy Jack Blackenship, James Wilcox, Kent McDonald, Andrew Hoeksema, Kent Thomas, Paul Barrett, Lily Jensen, Sarah Powell, Kurt Kroon, Pam Driesell, Brian McCutchen, Elizabeth Blood, Tiffany Bluhm, Wendy Wallin, Scotty Gullick, Sarah

Sanderson, Sam VanPykeren, Harmony Hookham-Dees, Caz Tod-Pearson, Jeff McSwain, Daniel Silliman, Mitchell Felton, Ross Murray, Kasey Ernst, and Aisea Taimani. And to those who are not named, who cannot be named at this time, I hold your stories close to my heart.

A huge thank-you to the team at Broadleaf Books. You believed this was a conversation the rest of us needed to have, so you said a hearty *yes* to teaming up and seeing it come to fruition. Lisa Kloskin, you are the editor dreams are made of. Thank you for listening when I needed it most, rewriting sentences when my brain lacked adequate functioning power, and patiently standing by when midnight revelations resulted in weeklong delays. My deepest thanks also goes to production editor Erin Gibbons and publicist Jana Nelson. Y'all went to *town* (or perhaps I should say, *to camp*) to see this book happen, and I, for one, am grateful.

Many hands (or creative minds, in this case) made the cover possible: Thanks for sticking with me on each and every design tweak, Carlos Esparza. And a huge thank-you to Peter Thomsen, Jason Boyett, and Margarette and John Kwok for your insights along the way.

To the gaggle of humans on Substack, Instagram, and Facebook who continue to find resonance in church camp writings, rantings, postings, and musings, it's a joy to find one another in the beauty and mess of life.

Thank you as well to the good folks at St. Paul's Episcopal in Oakland and in San Rafael and specifically to Fathers Mauricio Wilson and Christopher Martin: You have been home to me in this migration from one side of the Christian pond to the other. You share space with me, and you point me to love. Thank you to the tradition and the people who raised me and called me their own—your youth leaders, church staff, Young Life leaders, coworkers, camp summer staff members, and assignment teams taught me to love and be love in return. I am who I am because of your profound influence on my life.

The same goes for my family of origin: Dan, Noel, Brandon, and Aleah, you are the mayonnaise to my steamed artichoke, the garlic butter to my cracked crab. I'm grateful for the many memories we share, Strawberry Shortcake capes, family road trips down the I-5 corridor, and faith traditions alike. You anchor me to love, and I am grateful.

Finally, to the three who hold my heart, whom I share walls and beds and dinners around the table with too: James, Canon, and Theo, this book wouldn't be a reality without your patience, encouragement, and incredibly good looks. But mostly, thanks for eating a whole lot of buttered noodles and meat patties for dinner so I could hole away and write. Love you more.

Notes

Prologue

1 "Sacred playgrounds" is what Jacob Sorenson calls camps in a book with the same name. Jacob Sorenson, *Sacred Playgrounds* (Eugene, OR: Cascade Books, 2021).

2 This is what Richard Rohr calls God. "The Really Real," Center for Action and Contemplation, March 10, 2024, https://cac.org/daily-meditations/the-really-real/#:~:text=Richard%20Rohr%20invites%20us%20to,history%20a%20new%20social%20order.

3 The aforementioned sentence includes camps that happened through parachurch organizations and not through actual denominations. They may not have called themselves Bible camp, per se, but as you'll soon learn, I think it's safe to say they still operated as church camps in mission and scope.

4 Pairs well with the "things of this world."

5 This was, oh, how shall we say it, before the days of the internet. Sure, it was a thing, but it was also a really slow-modem type of thing. Cell phones were virtually nonexistent. So you didn't head to the internet for a job; you walked into the career counselor's office.
6 Mayflies live approximately twenty-four hours, which is to say that I gave the decision to work at camp about thirty-two seconds of thought, when all was said and done.
7 Accessed June 17, 2024, https://atascaderonews.com/news/honoring-rev-dr-martin-luther-king-jr/.
8 Accessed June 17, 2024, https://brittanytalissaking.medium.com/mlk-brought-us-into-the-light-8c2ac353ffb4.

Chapter 1: Welcome to Camp!

1 "converter (n.)," *Online Etymology Dictionary*, accessed June 17, 2024, https://www.etymonline.com/word/converter.
2 "converter (n.)," *Online Etymology Dictionary*.
3 Accessed June 17, 2024, https://www.instagram.com/p/Cmy97bgAVNE/?hl=en.
4 Susan Sontag, "Notes on 'Camp,'" https://monoskop.org/images/5/59/Sontag_Susan_1964_Notes_on_Camp.pdf.
5 All credit to riding the idea goes to the program team from whom I stole the original idea (Woodleaf, 2000), only to re-create it the next summer (Frontier Ranch, 2001).
6 "A History of Evangelism in the United States," *Brewminate*, June 28, 2020, https://brewminate.com/a-history-of-evangelicalism-in-the-united-states/.
7 Sorenson, *Sacred Playgrounds*, 19.
8 Nancy Ferguson and Jennifer Burch, "Religious Camps: Common Roots and New Sprouts," American Camp Association, November 1, 2011, https://www.acacamps.org/article/camping-magazine/religious-camps-common-roots-new-sprouts.
9 Ferguson and Burch, "Religious Camps."
10 Of note, small group interactions still play a major role at church camps across the United States today when campers spend a disproportionate amount of time with their cabinmates. These small groups sit together at meals and sleep in bunks next to one another;

they often wrestle through "cabin-time questions" as a group, sit with one another during programmed events, and bond over activities during the day.

11 "A History of Evangelism."

12 Katelyn Beaty, *Celebrities for Jesus* (Ada, MI: Baker Books, 2022), 25.

13 Kristin DuMez, *Jesus and John Wayne* (New York: Liveright, 2020), 29.

14 Sorenson, *Sacred Playgrounds*, 34.

15 Sorenson, *Sacred Playgrounds*, 37.

16 Sorenson, *Sacred Playgrounds*, 37.

17 Sorenson, *Sacred Playgrounds*, 37.

18 Jana Riess, "What's a 'White Evangelical' Anyway? It's Hard to Pin Down," Religion News Service, October 29, 2021, https://religionnews.com/2021/10/29/whats-a-white-evangelical-anyway-its-hard-to-pin-down/.

19 Riess, "What's a 'White Evangelical' Anyway?"

20 Riess, "What's a 'White Evangelical' Anyway?"

21 Riess, "What's a 'White Evangelical' Anyway?"

22 Felix James Miller, "Summer Camp: An Ailing American Institution," Public Discourse, August 14, 2023, https://www.thepublicdiscourse.com/2023/08/90569/.

23 Jared Stacy, "A History of the Culture Wars," April 5, 2021, https://jaredstacy.com/2021/04/05/a-history-of-the-culture-wars/.

24 Stacy, "A History of the Culture Wars."

25 Stacy, "A History of the Culture Wars."

26 Stacy, "A History of the Culture Wars."

27 Stacy, "A History of the Culture Wars."

28 Bizerko was a beloved game played at Cascades Camp in Yelm, Washington, as recalled by a former summer staff member.

29 Chris Staron, "S4:E3 Jesus and John Wayne," Truce Podcast, June 8, 2021, https://trucepodcast.com/tag/kristin-kobes-du-mez/.

30 Beaty, *Celebrities for Jesus*, 26.

31 Kristin Kobes Du Mez, *Jesus and John Wayne: How White Evangelicals Corrupted a Faith and Fractured a Nation* (2020), https://readingreligion.org/9781631495731/jesus-and-john-wayne/.

32 I have not found church camp happy hours to be a thing; however, it is a favored pastime at numerous churches across the country.

33 "Letters to the Editor," *Christianity Today*, September 7, 2012, https://www.christianitytoday.com/ct/2012/september/letters-to-the-editor.html.

34 Lisa Kadane, "The Benefits of Sending Your Kid to Overnight Camp," *Today's Parent*, July 5, 2021, https://www.todaysparent.com/family/activities/the-benefits-of-sending-your-kid-to-overnight-camp/.

35 Rachel Held Evans, "Opinion: Want Millennials Back in the Pews? Stop Trying to Make Church 'Cool,'" *Washington Post*, April 30, 2015, https://www.washingtonpost.com/opinions/jesus-doesnt-tweet/2015/04/30/fb07ef1a-ed01-11e4-8666-a1d756d0218e_story.html.

36 Evans, "Opinion."

37 Evans, "Opinion."

Chapter 2: God the Mostly Father

1 Lest you don't know what a Barcalounger is, it's right here: https://www.barcalounger.com.

2 "Four Spiritual Laws: The Basics Series," *Campus Ministry Today*, accessed June 17, 2024, https://campusministry.org/docs/tools/FourSpiritualLaws.pdf.

3 "Bill Bright," *Wikipedia*, accessed June 17, 2024, https://en.wikipedia.org/wiki/Bill_Bright.

4 Reports vary widely: some lowball the number and say only 100 million have received a tract, while others state over 4 billion tracts have been distributed. Seeing as Baptist Press seems to be the most legitimate of publications cited, I'm going with the 2.5 billion they quote. "Campus Crusade Founder Bill Bright Dies; 'Four Spiritual Laws' among Legacies," *Baptist Press*, July 21, 2003, https://www.baptistpress.com/resource-library/news/campus-crusade-founder-bill-bright-dies-four-spiritual-laws-among-legacies/.

5 "Blinded by the Bright," *Christian E-Books*, accessed June 17, 2024, http://www.christianebooks.com/blindedbythebright.htm#:~:text=making%20the%20theology%20of%20Bill,people%20raised%20in%20Christian%20homes.

6 Madeleine L'Engle, *A Circle of Quiet* (New York: HarperOne, 1984), 200.

7 *Middle-earth* is another name for New Zealand, in case you didn't know.

8 Ashley Easter, "How Patriarchy in the Church Plays a Role in Abuse," *Relevant Magazine*, March 21, 2022, https://relevant magazine.com/faith/church/3-ways-womens-equality-can-counteract -abuse/.

9 Actually, he probably wasn't allowed to be a girls' counselor . . . but if there's a will, there just might be a way.

10 In the Old Testament, Jezebel was the wife of Ahab, king of Israel. But because she fostered the worship of Baal and tried to kill the prophet Elijah, not only was *she* killed, but her name also became associated with a woman who is power-hungry, violent, and even whorish. I, for instance, was once called a Jezebel because I questioned a man in authority. Was I power-hungry? Doubtful. Violent or whorish? If going against the rules of the patriarchy is defined as such, then I guess I was *quite* the Jezebel.

11 "What Is Purity Culture?," Linda Kay Klein, accessed June 17, 2024, https://lindakayklein.com/what-is-purity-culture/.

12 "Purity Culture," *Women and Church*, accessed June 17, 2024, https://www.womenandchurch.com/purity-culture.

13 Cynthia and Susan, "Episode 112: What about Purity Culture? A Conversation with Colette Dalton," *At Last She Said It* podcast, accessed June 17, 2024, https://atlastshesaidit.org/episode-112-what-about -purity-culture-a-conversation-with-colette-dalton/.

14 A reference to Romans 14:13, as to "never put a stumbling block or hindrance in the way of a brother." What stumbling block were we preventing, though? Did we actually think a brother might trip and fall, their penis accidentally landing in a woman's vagina? It is possible, I suppose.

15 "What Is Purity Culture?"

16 William Shakespeare, *Twelfth Night*, Act II, scene 4, lines 42–45, https://www.folger.edu/explore/shakespeares-works/twelfth-night /read/2/4/.

17 According to the playwright's website, *Broken Heart* is said to have been seen by over three million youth worldwide.

18 *Broken Heart*, accessed June 17, 2024, https://vimeo.com/372 659178.

19 *Broken Heart*.

20 "The Story Behind the Broken Heart Play," Linda J. MacDonald, accessed June 17, 2024, https://www.lindajmacdonald.com/blog/2018/11/15/the-story-behind-the-broken-heart-play.
21 "The Story Behind the Broken Heart Play."
22 It should be said that "illicit sex" entirely meant *premarital sex.*
23 "What Is Purity Culture?"
24 In other words, don't have sex! No purple, boys and girls.
25 Bradley Onishi, *Preparing for War* (Minneapolis: Broadleaf, 2023).
26 Onishi, *Preparing for War.*
27 Onishi, *Preparing for War,* 112.
28 Amy Peeler, *Women and the Gender of God* (Grand Rapids, MI: Eerdmans, 2022), 9.
29 Peeler, *Women and the Gender of God,* 109.
30 Christena Cleveland, *God Is a Black Woman* (San Francisco: HarperOne, 2022), 15.

Chapter 3: Superhero Jesus

1 Deborah Jian Lee, *Rescuing Jesus* (Boston: Beacon Press, 2015), 62.
2 This was specifically about gender discrimination toward a camp, but the same applies given the nonprofit status: Michael A. Blickman, "Single-Gender Camps and Hiring Employees: Is Gender an Appropriate Hiring Criterion?," American Camp Association, February 1, 2004, https://www.acacamps.org/article/campline/single-gender-camps-hiring-employees-gender-appropriate-hiring-criterion.
3 Jian Lee, *Rescuing Jesus,* 68.
4 "A Christian Camp Said a Transgender Child Couldn't Stay in a Boys' Cabin. Then Came the Human Rights Battle," August 14, 2022, https://www.cbc.ca/news/canada/new-brunswick/caton-summer-camp-transgender-1.6549560.
5 "Counselor Fired from Bellingham Religious Camp for Being Gay," June 23, 2019, https://www.kiro7.com/news/local/bellingham-teen-fired-as-christian-camp-counselor-because-he-is-gay/958279965/.
6 Eliel Cruz, "Why Christian Summer Camps Should Stop Rejecting LGBT Counselors, Campers," Religion News Service, June 4,

2015, https://religionnews.com/2015/06/04/why-christian-summer-camps-should-stop-rejecting-lgbt-counselors-campers/.

7 Author interview with Sam VanPykeren, September 8, 2023.

8 Cruz, "Why Christian Summer Camps."

9 Cruz, "Why Christian Summer Camps."

10 "A Camper's Prayer," accessed June 17, 2015, https://www.thenamingproject.org.

11 Evans, "Opinion."

12 Erin S. Lane, *Lessons in Belonging from a Church-Going Commitment Phobe* (Westmont, IL: IVP, 2015), 25.

13 Lisa Sharon Harper, *Fortune* (Ada, MI: Brazos Press, 2022), 30.

14 Shane Claiborne, *Rethinking Life* (Grand Rapids, MI: Zondervan, 2023), 156.

15 Acts: 16:31.

16 Beth Birmingham and Eeva Sallinen Simard, *Creating Cultures of Belonging* (Westmont, IL: IVP, 2015), 10.

17 Michael Frost and Alan Hirsch, *The Shaping of Things to Come* (Carol Stream, IL: Tyndale House, 2003), 68.

18 "Who's In and Who's Out? (Bounded vs. Centered Sets)," Church Leaders, March 14, 2011, https://churchleaders.com/smallgroups/small-group-blogs/149608-whos_in_and_whos_out_bounded_vs_centered_sets.html.

19 Emily Dickinson, "Life—Is What We Make of It," 698, accessed July 15, 2024, https://allpoetry.com/Lifeis-what-we-make-of-it.

20 In *Love Wins*, Rob Bell writes, "Love demands that they belong." Rob Bell, *Love Wins* (San Francisco: HarperOne, 2012), 64. He was talking about past experiences of faith that may not align with current beliefs. Here, we're talking about the very personhoods of every human to have graced this earth. In both cases, love demands belonging.

21 John 1:14, *The Message.*

22 Galatians 5:22–23.

23 This is a twist on the Iona Invitation, a communion prayer: "The table of bread and wine is now to be made ready. So come to this table, you who have much faith and you who would like to have more; you who are here for the first time; you who have been here often; you who have not been for a long time; you who have tried to follow Jesus and you who have failed; come. It is Christ

himself who invites us to meet him here." From the bulletin of All Saints Episcopal Church, San Leandro, CA, December 10, 2023.

Chapter 4: Dirty Rotten Little Sinners

1 Did you catch the penultimate nod toward penal substitution's number-one verse? Romans 3:23, baby.

2 Romans 6:23, entirely ignoring the second part of the verse altogether, "But the gift of God is eternal life in Christ Jesus."

3 I am slightly taking Luther's words out of context, given that he said them about himself on proclaiming the gospel: "I desire above all things that my name should be concealed, and that none be called by the name of Lutheran; but of Christian. What is Luther? My doctrine is not mine, but Christ's. I was not crucified for any. How comes it to pass, that I, who am but a filthy, stinking bag of worms; that any of the sons of God should be denominated from my name? Away with these schismatical names! Let us be denominated from Christ, from whom alone we have our doctrine."

4 Jonathan Edwards, "Sinners in the Hands of an Angry God," part I of paragraph, accessed July 15, 2024, https://www.blueletterbible.org/Comm/edwards_jonathan/Sermons/Sinners.cfm.

5 "Human Depravity," *Oxford Dictionary*, accessed July 15, 2024, https://books.google.com/books?id=anecAQAAQBAJ&pg=PA1878&lpg=PA1878&dq=—"the+Calvinist+doctrine+that+human+nature+is+thoroughly+corrupt+and+sinful+as+a+result+of+the+Fall,"+oxford&source=bl&ots=T0dCgwkEBM&sig=ACfU3U2_Egj7yIw7amRqxC7KIaccKX5CWg&hl=en&sa=X&ved=2ahUKEwjdmqPX6omHAxWPgo4IHRlnD8YQ6AF6BAgjEAM#v=onepage&q=—"the%20Calvinist%20doctrine%20that%20human%20nature%20is%20thoroughly%20corrupt%20and%20sinful%20as%20a%20result%20of%20the%20Fall%2C"%20oxford&f=false.

6 Bell, *Love Wins*, 64.

7 Thomas Schreiner, "Substitutionary Atonement," The Gospel Coalition, accessed June 17, 2024, https://www.thegospelcoalition.org/essay/substitutionary-atonement/.

8 Schreiner, "Substitutionary Atonement."

9 Brian Arnold, "Did the Church Fathers Affirm Penal Substitutionary Atonement?," 9Marks, August 20, 2019, https://www.9marks.org/article/did-the-church-fathers-affirm-penal-substitutionary-atonement/#:~:text=Since%20the%20Reformation%2C%20Protestants%20have,place%20and%20paid%20our%20penalty.

10 Scott J. Higgins, "Why We Need to Move Away from Substitutionary Atonement," October 23, 2013, https://scottjhiggins.com/why-we-need-to-move-away-from-substitutionary-atonement/.

11 Brian McLaren, "Q & R: Penal Substitutionary Atonement," March 14, 2012, http://brianmclaren.net/q-r-penal-substitutionary-atonement/.

12 Jo Luehmann, "Abusive Theology (Penal Substitutionary Atonement)," Facebook, accessed June 17, 2024, https://www.facebook.com/watch/?v=903687307033184.

13 Dr. Laura E. Anderson, "What Is Religious Trauma?" accessed June 17, 2024, https://drlauraeanderson.com/blog/religious-trauma.

14 Anderson, "What Is Religious Trauma?"

15 Anderson, "What Is Religious Trauma?"

16 "Carrot and stick," *Wikipedia*, accessed June 17, 2024, https://en.wikipedia.org/wiki/Carrot_and_stick.

17 Bradley Jersak, *Her Gates Will Never Be Shut* (Eugene, OR: Wipf and Stock Publishers, 2005), 188.

18 Jersak, *Her Gates Will Never Be Shut*, 201.

19 Jersak suggests these three main viewpoints on hell in his book *Her Gates Will Never Be Shut*. Not to be forgotten, the book *Four Views of Hell* introduced readers to four different views of hell: literal, purgatorial, conditional, and metaphorical.

20 Saint Augustine, *City of God: Book XX* (Peabody, MA: Hendrickson Publishers, 2009), chap. 1.

21 Jersak, *Her Gates Will Never Be Shut*, 142.

22 Edwards, "Sinners in the Hands of an Angry God," part II of paragraph. It should be said that I don't entirely despise the writing of Jonathan Edwards. I can't get enough of this line, for instance: "Lord, stamp eternity on my eyeballs." Or of this goal: "Resolution One: I will live for God. Resolution Two: If no one else does, I still will." Still, I wouldn't exactly call him my homeboy.

23 "Guest Post: 10 Good, Clean Messy Games," accessed June 17, 2024, https://blog.downloadyouthministry.com/guest-post-10

-good-clean-messy-games/—also, I'm not sure why he said "lives of students lives" or didn't believe in a possessive apostrophe after *students*, but maybe that's just me.

24 Jeff McSwain, "Young Life and the Gospel of All-Along Belonging," *The Other Journal*, Issue 17: Economics, accessed June 17, 2024, https://theotherjournal.com/2010/01/young-life-and-the-gospel-of-all-along-belonging/.

25 McSwain, "Young Life and the Gospel."

26 Psalm 107:2–3.

27 I am happy to report that when Jeff left Young Life, he had strong community support. With the backing of a new board of directors (a board, I should add, that followed him from his previous role in Young Life), Jeff formed Reality Ministries, an organization based in Durham, North Carolina. According to their website, although the original vision was "for all staff, volunteers, and participants to grow together in the truth that the deepest reality of life is God's love for every person in Jesus Christ," the ministry now focuses on "building community with the overlooked and underserved populations in Durham, beginning with those with developmental disabilities." For Jeff, he's simply leaned into the reality had been there all along. "History," Reality Ministries, accessed June 17, 2024, https://realityministriesinc.org/history/.

28 Part of this story originally appeared in a devotion for *Forward Day by Day* (Cincinnati: Forward Movement, December 2021), 38.

29 Jersak, *Her Gates Will Never Be Shut*, 164.

30 Oliver Slow, "Why Has the Gaza Ceasefire Come to an End?," BBC, December 1, 2023, https://www.bbc.com/news/world-middle-east-67589259#.

31 Riff on 1 Corinthians 5:17, *The Message.*

32 Anne Lamott, *Dusk, Night, Dawn* (New York: Riverhead Books, 2021), 84.

Chapter 5: Cry Night

1 Facts about Charing Cross: "Charing Cross," *Wikipedia*, accessed June 17, 2024, https://en.wikipedia.org/wiki/Charing_Cross.

2 Max Lucado, *Grace for the Moment, Volume II* (Nashville: Thomas Nelson, 2006), 110.

3 N. T. Wright, *The Day the Revolution Began* (San Francisco: HarperOne, 2018), 9.

4 Wright, *The Day the Revolution Began*, 22.

5 A truncated retelling of the Nicene Creed, y'all.

6 Howard Thurman, *The Mood of Christmas* (Richmond, IN: Friends United Press, 1985), 12.

7 Matthew 27:46.

8 "The Dogs of Good Friday," *The Corners by Nadia Bolz-Weber*, April 10, 2020, https://thecorners.substack.com/p/the-dogs-of-good-friday#:~:text=It%20is%20as%20if%20the,we%20need%20a%20protective%20barrier.

9 This section on Matthew 27:46 comes from a homily delivered at St. Paul's Episcopal Church, Oakland, on Good Friday, April 7, 2023.

10 Wright, *The Day the Revolution Began*, 42.

11 Wright, *The Day the Revolution Began*, 43.

12 Wright, *The Day the Revolution Began*, 43.

13 Wright, *The Day the Revolution Began*, 39.

14 Interlude originally titled "An Echo of Salvation, Written at Collegeville Writing Institute with Mary Potter," October 2018.

15 Merriam-Webster, "emotionality," accessed July 15, 2024, https://www.merriam-webster.com/dictionary/emotionality.

16 Chris Drew, "10 Groupthink Examples (Plus Definition & Critique)," Helpful Professor, May 17, 2023, https://helpfulprofessor.com/groupthink-examples/.

17 Drew, "10 Groupthink Examples."

18 Roland Bal, "Why You Are Being Manipulated to Groupthink," accessed June 17, 2024, https://rolandbal.com/why-you-are-being-manipulated-to-groupthink/.

19 Thank you, Kurt Kroon, for this timeshare presentation analogy.

20 Roman Empire quote and two sentences that follow: "First Sunday of Christmas," December 31, 2023, https://www.workingpreacher.org/commentaries/revised-common-lectionary/first-sunday-of-christmas-2/commentary-on-luke-222-40-7. Part of this was quoted in a sermon (preached by me) on December 31, 2023, at St. Paul's Episcopal Church in Oakland, California.

21 Richard Rohr, "Jesus and the Cross," Wisdom2Be, accessed June 17, 2024, https://www.wisdom2be.com/essays-insights-wisdom writings-spirituality/jesus-and-the-cross-by-richard-rohr.
22 Rohr, "Jesus and the Cross."
23 Rohr, "Jesus and the Cross."
24 Rohr, "Jesus and the Cross."
25 Rohr, "Jesus and the Cross."
26 Rohr, "Jesus and the Cross."
27 Sara Billups, *Orphaned Believers* (Grand Rapids, MI: Baker Books, 2023), 131.

Chapter 6: Side Note, Rose Again

1 *Talladega Nights*, of course.
2 "Wait a minute," you might be saying. "Are you sure it was actually a bear you encountered outside your tent? You didn't exactly see a bear, correct?" That is correct. Next question, please.
3 As the aphorism plainly states, "Fish and visitors smell in three days."
4 Zane Pratt, "What Is Conversion and Why Does It Matter?," IMB, September 1, 2016, https://www.imb.org/2016/09/01/20160907what-is-conversion-and-why-does-it-matter/#:~:text=Conversion%20is%20the%20divinely%20enabled,Savior%20and%20Lord%20(believe).
5 David Fitch, "The Emerging View of Salvation: Brian McLaren and the Danger of De-eschatologizing the Kingdom," Missio Alliance, June 28, 2010, https://www.missioalliance.org/the-emerging-view-of-salvation-brian-mclaren-and-the-danger-of-de-eschatologizing-the-kingdom/.
6 This is essentially the premise of Wright's book *Surprised by Hope*, as well as a clear idea in *The Day the Revolution Began*. I don't believe it's a direct quote as much as an understanding of Wright's works.
7 Depeche Mode, "Personal Jesus," 1990. But, oh, it's such a good song.
8 Fitch, "The Emerging View of Salvation."
9 "Remembering the Future," Spring 2008, https://spu.edu/depts/uc/response/spring2k8/features/remembering-the-future.asp.
10 "Remembering the Future."

11 "Remembering the Future."

12 Calvinist Cadet Corps, accessed June 17, 2024, https://www.calvinistcadets.org.

13 Although the acronym will live in my heart forever, the specific wording after the fact came from this website: accessed June 17, 2024, https://www.myvscog.org/abcs-of-salvation/.

14 "In Christ Alone (My Hope Is Found)," Song by Adrienne Camp and Geoff Moore and The Distance, 2002, https://www.stuarttownend.co.uk/song/in-christ-alone/.

15 "Our Story," Billy Graham Training Center at The Cove, accessed June 17, 2024, https://thecove.org/our-story/.

16 Billups, *Orphaned Believers*, 188.

17 Martin Soto, "Best Christian Summer Camps for Kids and Families 2024," Summer Camp Hub, accessed June 17, 2024, https://summercamphub.com/christian-summer-camps/. This was also compared with the similarly titled "Best Christian Summer Camps: Jennifer Betts"; "Best Christian Summer Camps," Love to Know, March 13, 2019, https://www.lovetoknow.com/parenting/teens/best-christian-summer-camps.

18 Kelly Mahoney, "Top Summer Camps for Christian Teens," *Learn Religions*, March 10, 2019, https://www.learnreligions.com/top-summer-camps-for-christian-teens-712593.

19 Megan Fowler, "Welcome to Christian Camps' Weirdest, Hardest Summer," *Christianity Today*, June 22, 2020, https://www.christianitytoday.com/ct/2020/july-august/christian-summer-camp-cancel-coronavirus-pandemic.html.

20 Mallory Challis, "From Isolation to Ministerial Pasta, How Summer Camp Has Changed since COVID Showed Up," *Baptist News Global*, June 27, 2023, https://baptistnews.com/article/from-isolation-to-ministerial-pasta-how-summer-camp-has-changed-since-covid-showed-up/.

21 Camp Cho-Yeh does not offer one-week camps for this age group. This was calculated based on a two-week stay divided in half. Accessed June 17, 2024, https://cho-yeh.org/dates-rates/.

22 The camp lists that a week at camp is worth $1,599, but they slashed the price to $1,299. Required deposit and optional monthly payment plans available. Accessed June 17, 2024, https://www.pinecove.com/summer-camps/overnight-youth-camps/.

23 Accessed June 17, 2024, https://kanakuk.com/k-seven/.

24 Accessed June 17, 2024, https://campozark.com/program/.

25 Yosemite Sierra does not actually offer one-week camps. This was calculated based on what a two-week camp would cost were it divided in half. Accessed June 17, 2024, https://yssc.com/california-christian-summer-camp/#dates.

26 Jake Sorenson, "The Lasting Impact of Christian Summer Camp," Building Faith, June 5, 2017, https://buildfaith.org/lasting-impact-christian-summer-camp/.

27 Aaron Helman, "Why Church Camp Is a Harder Sell Than Ever and What You Can Do about It," *Ministry to Youth*, accessed June 17, 2024, https://ministrytoyouth.com/why-church-camp-is-a-harder-sell-than-ever-and-what-you-can-do-about-it/.

28 Fowler, "Welcome to Christian Camps'."

29 Fowler, "Welcome to Christian Camps'."

30 Fowler, "Welcome to Christian Camps'."

31 Challis, "From Isolation to Ministerial Pasta."

32 As you'll soon see, if the average pay for summer staff equates to $2.96 an hour, the yearly pay would be equivalent to $5,920. In the United States, the amount for an individual at poverty level is $15,060. So summer staffers are making $9,140 less than poverty level (or 39.3 percent of the threshold, which is 60.7 percent less).

33 Line taken from the following random camp website: accessed June 17, 2024, https://www.campzephyr.org/summer-staff.

34 This was based on the average pay rate offered to counselors at the five camps also listed above: Camp Cho-Yeh: training: $100, $250/week, up to $3,000 for 12 weeks; Pine Cove Camp: $2,200 for the whole summer (11 weeks)—$200/week; Kanakuk Kamp: $900–$1,300 for 4–6 weeks of work (so $1,800–$2,600 for closer to 11 or 12 weeks)—$1,100 average, $220/week; Camp Ozark: $1,550, $258/week; Yosemite Sierra: $301/week.

35 In this scenario, staff is working the following hours: Sunday: 1–10 p.m. (nine hours), Monday: 7 a.m.–10 p.m. (fourteen hours), Tuesday: 7 a.m.–10 p.m. (fourteen hours), Wednesday: 7 a.m.–10 p.m. (fourteen hours), Thursday: 7 a.m.–10 p.m. (fourteen hours), Friday: 7 a.m.–10 p.m. (fourteen hours), Saturday: 7–11 a.m. (four hours). This is not an unheard of schedule.

36 Eighty-three hours/week = $2.96 an hour, or $41/day, if you base it on a 6-day schedule in which staff receive 24 hours off.

37 In general, housing is priced at 30 percent and meals at 10 percent. This was confirmed through one camp's website: Yosemite Sierra pays its summer staff $301/week, but if you include room and board, which is valued at $510/week, the salary is 59 percent of what the individual is actually making. That being said, if college students were actually receiving a $510/week paycheck, according to our calculations, their hourly rate would go up to $6.07 an hour. Paid at this rate, the yearly salary increases to $12,140/year, which is still below the poverty rate but getting closer to prosperity! US Poverty guidelines are here: "Poverty Guidelines," Assistant Secretary for Planning and Evaluation, accessed June 17, 2024, https://aspe.hhs.gov/topics/poverty-economic-mobility/poverty-guidelines.

38 FCA, "Be a Huddle Leader," accessed June 17, 2024, https://www.fcacamps.org/campstaff/.

39 This is just one example of high school students paying to work at camp: "Leaders in Training (LITs)," accessed January 14, 2024, https://frontier-ranch.com/high-school/lit/.

40 Rachel Premack, "The $500 Million Christian Camp Giant Young Life Has Failed to Protect Young People from Sexual Misconduct, Some Former Members Say," *Business Insider*, October 7, 2021, https://www.businessinsider.com/young-life-sexual-misconduct-claims-christian-camps-2021-10.

41 Anne Paddock, "Where Does $100 to Young Life Go?," *Paddock Post*, August 14, 2020, https://paddockpost.com/2020/08/14/where-does-100-to-young-life-go/.

42 Young Life mission statement: "Mission and Values of Young Life," accessed June 17, 2024, https://jobs.younglife.org/mission-and-values-of-young-life/.

43 Erin Jean Warde, *Sober Spirituality* (Grand Rapids, MI: Brazos Press, 2023), 149.

44 Jian Lee, *Rescuing Jesus*, 178.

45 Walter Brueggemann, *Money and Possessions* (Louisville, KY: Westminster John Knox Press, 2016), xxi.

46 Brueggemann, *Money and Possessions*, 115.

47 Sorenson, *Sacred Playgrounds*, 10.

48 Read this for more on the "reset" button many camps took: "Emergent Camp Trends," American Camp Association, March 11, 2021, https://www.acacamps.org/article/camping-magazine/emergent-camp-trends.

49 Tricia Hersey, *Rest Is Resistance* (New York: Little, Brown Spark), 75.

50 God is bigger than if/then statements, and I just made an if/then statement.

Chapter 7: Now Go and Live the (White) Way of Jesus

1 Even though the national figure is spelled "McGruff," my family paid homage to the "Mac" of our Scottish roots.

2 Just a reminder, y'all: at this time in my life, God was still a "he," every single pronoun included.

3 *The Fox and the Hound*, of course. Walt Disney Pictures, 1981.

4 Liz Tichenor, *The Night Lake* (Berkeley: Counterpoint Press, 2021), 260.

5 Richard Rohr, *Yes, and: Daily Meditation* (Cincinnati: Franciscan Media, 2019), 68.

6 The skit was called "On the Fence," and the real clincher was when the narrator asked, "Which side do you choose?" And before the guy in the middle could get a word in edgewise, the devil said, "Well, I own the fence." Decisions!

7 "Conformity," *Wikipedia*, accessed June 17, 2024, https://en.wikipedia.org/wiki/Conformity.

8 Acts 8:26–40.

9 Debie Thomas, "When All Are Welcome," *Journey with Jesus*, April 25, 2021, https://www.journeywithjesus.net/essays/2995-when-all-are-welcome.

10 Thomas, "When All Are Welcome," 1.

11 Accessed June 17, 2024, https://www.foresthome.org/camps-and-retreats/youth-summer-camp/.

12 Accessed June 17, 2024, https://www.campbarakel.org/events/summer-ms.

13 "This Is the Best Week of Your Life," 2018, https://www.facebook.com/YoungLife/videos/10156552206367370/.

14 Sorenson, *Sacred Playgrounds*, 27.

15 "Timeline of ACA and Summer Camp," American Camp Association, accessed June 17, 2024, https://www.acacamps.org/about/history/timeline.

16 "Timeline of ACA and Summer Camp."

17 “Black Codes,” *History*, March 29, 2023, https://www.history.com/topics/black-history/black-codes.

18 The Voting Rights Act prohibited racial discrimination in voting, of course.

19 Sorenson, *Sacred Playgrounds*, 28.

20 Sorenson, *Sacred Playgrounds*, 28.

21 Sorenson, *Sacred Playgrounds*, 29.

22 Nancy Ferguson and Jennifer Burch, “Religious Camps: Common Roots and New Sprouts,” American Camp Association, November 1, 2011, https://www.acacamps.org/article/camping-magazine/religious-camps-common-roots-new-sprouts.

23 “CAMPCOUNTS 2020,” American Camp Association, accessed June 17, 2024, https://www.acacamps.org/sites/default/files/resource_library/research/CampCounts2020-Report_2-12.pdf.

24 “CAMPCOUNTS 2020.”

25 Sorenson, *Sacred Playgrounds*, 29.

26 Bob Ditter, “Race and Camp: Creating an Environment in Camp Communities That Is Truly Welcoming to People of Color,” American Camp Association, September 1, 2020, https://www.acacamps.org/article/camping-magazine/race-camp-creating-environment-camp-communities-truly-welcoming-people-color.

27 Rogelio Sáenz and Dudley L. Poston Jr., “Children of Color Already Make Up the Majority of Kids in Many US States,” *The Conversation*, January 9, 2020, https://theconversation.com/children-of-color-already-make-up-the-majority-of-kids-in-many-us-states-128499.

28 “Camp Is for Black Kids,” Camp in the Community, February 25, 2022, https://www.campinthecommunity.org/post/camp-is-for-black-kids.

29 Anthea Butler, *White Evangelical Racism* (Chapel Hill: University of North Carolina Press, 2021), 9.

30 Butler, *White Evangelical Racism*, 9.

31 “Camp Is for Black Kids.”

32 Holden Conference Center is part of the United Methodist Church, accessed June 17, 2024, http://www.holstoncamping.com.

33 “Camp Is for Black Kids.”

34 “Camp Is for Black Kids.” Danaya did not respond to requests to interview; however, camp leadership responded with the following note: “It excites me that your work may help illuminate the

problems of the past (and present in so many places) so that we can work toward a more equitable and inclusive world at camp and beyond."

35 Mitchell Felton, "Do You Want to Be Better?," Do Better Young Life, accessed June 17, 2024, https://dobetteryounglife.com/dbylblog/doyouwanttobebetter.

36 Felton, "Do You Want to Be Better?"

37 Accessed June 17, 2024, https://campkanuga.org.

38 "Camp Bob," accessed June 17, 2024, https://www.kanuga.org/camps-outdoor-education/camp-bob-kanuga/.

39 It should also be noted that a lot of camps prize themselves on nicknames; campers never know staff members' "real" names, only their camp names. It's a thing.

40 This is what Sorenson calls church camps. I love it, personally.

41 Victoria Loorz, *Church of the Wild* (Minneapolis: Broadleaf Books, 2021), 105.

42 This is *ubuntu!* And that sentence and the one that follows are two sentences from a sermon I preached on June 13, 2022, at St. Paul's Episcopal Church in San Rafael, California.

43 "Camp Is for Black Kids."

44 Accessed June 17, 2024, https://rescuereleaserestore.org.

45 "North Bay Camp Gives Jewish Children of Color a Haven to Be Different Together," August 11, 2023, https://www.cbsnews.com/amp/sanfrancisco/news/north-bay-camp-jewish-children-color-haven-different-together/.

46 Accessed June 17, 2024, https://globaljews.org/camp/.

47 "Bridge Builders," accessed June 17, 2024, https://www.elcalivingwater.com/bridgebuilders/.

Epilogue

1 Thank you, Kurt Kroon, for first sharing this story with me. It came out anew when I went back to camp!